DATE DUE MAR 04

6/01/04			
GAYLORD			PRINTED IN U.S.A.

GOING WILD

GOING WILD

ADVENTURES WITH BIRDS
IN THE SUBURBAN
WILDERNESS

Robert Winkler

NATIONAL GEOGRAPHIC

WASHINGTON, D.C.

Published by the National Geographic Society

First printing, August 2003
Printed in U.S.A.
Design by Melissa Farris

Library of Congress Cataloging-in-Publication Data

Winkler, Robert, 1953-
  Going wild : adventures with birds in the suburban wilderness / Robert
Winkler.
      p. cm.
  ISBN 0-7922-6168-2
  1. Birds--Northeastern States. 2. Bird-watching--Northeastern States.
3. Winkler, Robert, 1953- I. Title.
  QL683.N73W56 2003
  598'.0974--dc21

                        2003014405

One of the world's largest nonprofit scientific and educational organizations, the National Geographic Society was founded in 1888 "for the increase and diffusion of geographic knowledge." Fulfilling this mission, the Society educates and inspires millions every day through its magazines, books, television programs, videos, maps and atlases, research grants, the National Geographic Bee, teacher workshops, and innovative class-room materials.

    The Society is supported through membership dues, charitable gifts, and income from the sale of its educational products. This support is vital to National Geographic's mission to increase global under-standing and promote conservation of our planet through exploration, research, and education.

For more information, please call 1-800-NGS LINE (647-5463) or write to the following address:
National Geographic Society
1145 17th Street N.W.
Washington, D.C. 20036-4688 U.S.A.

Visit the Society's Web site at www.nationalgeographic.com.

To Charlotte Byer Winkler

CONTENTS

ONE CAN HAVE NATURE ADVENTURES WITHOUT TRAVELING TO THE Serengeti or the Amazon. On walks in the unpeopled parts of the suburbs, I've witnessed the same wild creatures, struggles for survival, and natural beauty that we associate with true wilderness. As Henry David Thoreau, the original suburban nature writer, observed, "It is remarkable how many creatures live wild and free though secret in the woods, and sustain themselves in the neighborhood of towns."

At 18, I moved from Queens, New York, to southwestern Connecticut. More than 30 years have passed since then. I've logged tens of thousands of foot miles perambulating the wild places that most of my neighbors overlook, right here in suburban Fairfield County, 50 to 75 miles from New York City. I've come to know the area well, yet I never tire of my old haunts. I'm still learning secrets of animal behavior, and now and then I find a new place to explore.

Drawing on personal experience, I write about the birds of southern New England—hawks, eagles, owls, woodcocks, shrikes, warblers, thrushes—the same birds that occur over much of North America and, in a few cases, on other continents. I gather material by strapping on my boots, going into the woods and fields, and opening my senses.

I write about birds because they show the wild in all its glory, and they're easy to find. As such, they may be nature's best representatives. The study of birds is stimulating—challenging enough to be a lifelong pursuit, but not so challenging as to be beyond the average person's scope. My interest in birds, however, has not closed my eyes to other aspects of nature. This book includes essays on flying squirrels, copperheads, a woodland waterfall, a black spruce bog, and an observation or two on that sometimes peculiar subspecies of *Homo sapiens,* the suburbanite. I also recount a few adventures that took me beyond Fairfield County's borders.

This is a book for all readers, whether they are scientifically or spiritually inclined (or both). I have studied ornithology books, but I have heeded Walt Whitman's words: "You must not know too much, or be too precise or scientific about birds and trees and flowers and water-craft; a certain free margin, and even vagueness—perhaps ignorance, credulity—helps your enjoyment of these things."

Nature in the suburbs is fragmented hence this book is episodic. Readers can dip into chapters as they please with little sacrifice of coherence, just as a naturalist dips into this or that wildlife sanctuary. My favorite places—Wakeman's Farm, Sherwood Island State Park, the Saugatuck Reservoir, and the Paugusset State Forest—will keep popping up, as will the towns I've lived in: Westport, Weston, and Newtown.

Because I write about the birds of one of the richest counties in America, some people get the impression that I'm a country squire. Truth is, I've lived my entire adult life in small apartments, the last two carved out of sections of other people's houses. My present abode is a one-bedroom basement apartment. It's quiet, and through the glass door I look out on six bird feeders and a stream. I couldn't ask for more.

As the world grows more populous and technologically sophisticated, people seem to have a greater yearning to connect with the wild. In a sense, this is a how-to book in which I try to show a way to make that connection through birds. If I can do so living in one of the most densely populated counties in the United States, my bet is that you can, too.

CHAPTER I

BEARINGS

*Let the waters bring forth abundantly the moving
creature that hath life, and fowl that may fly above
the earth in the open firmament of heaven.*
GENESIS

A NEWSPAPER COLUMNIST WHERE I LIVE, IN AN ATTEMPT AT HUMOR, once complained in print that birds are noisy, flying nuisances that wake him at dawn and dirty his car. He saw no good reason for birds and suggested they be eliminated. He ridiculed birders like me as naturalistic oddballs who parade around the woods in paramilitary getups. A golfer, he proclaimed that birding has about as much sport as watching grass grow.

In a letter to the editor, I explained why birds deserve our respect, and why we birders watch them. Birds are important for a simple reason: They are here. Yes, they control insects, but their benefit to humanity is no more the measure of their worth than the pharmacy shelf is the measure of the tropical rain forest. Wildlife has a right to exist for its own sake. The height of species-ism would be to suggest that nature's profound creations must justify their presence to us. As if it were our place to grant birds permission to live!

As for birders, we are not frail, bookish fanatics in pith helmets and safari jackets. We dress like other people who frequent the woods, adding binoculars and perhaps a field guide. We don't do back flips at the sight of a Yellow-bellied Sapsucker (not east of the Rockies, anyway, where the species is not particularly unusual). When I go birding, I usually hike for miles, and I bird several times a week year-round, regardless of the weather. Watching birds, I have gained admittance to the secret society of the wild.

Like the best sports, birding challenges the physique, the senses, and the intellect. To see birds in all their wondrous forms, you would have to visit the wetlands, the coast, the open ocean, the mountaintop, the desert, the prairie, the jungle, the river rapids, the tundra, and the polar regions. When billions of birds migrate across North America—returning to northern breeding areas in spring and departing in fall for winter homes as far away as South America—birders around the country go afield to witness the mysterious and inspiring spectacle.

Why do people go out of their way to find birds? Birds are beautiful to look at, they make an incredible variety of sounds, and they exhibit fascinating behavior. Sighting a rare bird is as thrilling as finding the most precious gem. Birds come in all colors, and here in the United States they range in size from the 3.25-inch-long Calliope Hummingbird to the California Condor, with a wingspan that can exceed nine feet. Whether a bird's song is short and sweet or long and musical, virtually all bird songs are memorable and stirring.

Birds, in short, reflect nature's astounding diversity, and watching birds is nothing less than a celebration of life. But I think the real fascination with birds is that, more than any other creatures, they embody a freedom and wildness of which we humans can only dream. These colorful feathered sprites defy gravity at will. They go wherever they want, whenever they choose, some at lightning speed.

Living in humanity's overpopulated, paved-over world—with all its rules, regulations, and traffic jams—I think we envy the birds their wild freedom. We want it for ourselves, and so we birders watch, listen to, identify, count, list, house, feed, and photograph birds. They are more beautiful and exotic than any extraterrestrial being Hollywood could concoct, and yet they are here, at our doorsteps, for us to enjoy.

ARE THERE MOURNING DOVES IN QUEENS? ALTHOUGH I HAVE LIVED there for my first 18 years, I don't know. In all that time, I never saw or heard any. They must occur somewhere in that borough, which in area is New York City's largest. Widespread and common—the most abundant North American member of its family—the Mourning Dove lives year-round in all but the most northern of the lower 48 states. *Bull's Birds of New York State* describes it as breeding in "great numbers" on Long Island. Our house was on the borough's uncitified edge, about a mile from the Nassau County line. The Mourning Dove, however, prefers open suburbs to the sprawling checkerboard of 40-by-100-foot housing lots that characterized the neighborhood.

It is one of many common birds absent from my childhood. Indeed, I have few distinct memories of wild birds in Queens. I thought that if a bird was black, it must be a crow. Blue Jays, a rare sight on 248th Street, were to my mind bluebirds of happiness. There was a tame House Sparrow—I remember sitting in a circle with other children when it flew in and landed next to me. For two days the sparrow, which we named Tom, joined our sidewalk games. We accepted Tom as a playmate, never thinking that he wanted food. After I became interested in birds, I realized we had misjudged the sparrow in another way. Tom was a female.

An owl, of all things, also resides deep in my childhood memory. I went to see it with another boy. How we heard about it I can't recall. We crossed the street and walked up the block to the policeman's house. The owl, or an owl's image, stared out from a small open window at the peak of the garage. It didn't seem alive; it stood motionless, like a cutout. I can't recall it clearly enough to identify the species. No one was around to explain this oddity. I walked away puzzled.

Queens never made me into a bird lover because there weren't enough birds in my neighborhood to love. The postwar housing boom had created a pleasantly sterile environment. Each house had its patch of front lawn, its single tree on the aisle of grass between the sidewalk and the curb, its Lilliputian backyard framed by a chain-link fence. The house next door was hardly more than a couple of body lengths away.

The only sizable park in the area, Alley Pond, lay beyond my short walking range, and in my fearful child's imagination, lions and tigers roamed its woods. In time I learned that big cats wouldn't stalk me there, but my aversion stuck. Even as a teenager, I rarely went to the one place that could have held a variety of birds.

By no means did I feel deprived. I had all the diversions of a New York boyhood, including a three-speed bicycle, stickball games in the driveway, basketball games under garage-mounted rims, the candy store on Union Turnpike. A more mature and sensitive youth might have been able to respond to the faint call of the wild in the old neighborhood. I needed more to cross that threshold. I found it on a cul-de-sac in Westport, Connecticut.

While on Christmas break from college, I stayed alone at the Westport house—a small ranch on what seemed an extravagant 1.25-acre lot—the night before we moved in. Wrapped in my sleeping bag on the floor of the living room, I felt as if I were in a deserted hunting lodge. There was a fireplace and a large kitchen. Through the picture window I could make out the weeping willow in the center of the panoramic front lawn.

Earlier I had surveyed the grounds. The deciduous woods on three sides of the house contained big trees, fallen trees, brushy undergrowth, thick vines, and leaf litter. There was a house to the left and another across the street, but set on one-acre lots themselves, they seemed very far away. I felt profound tranquillity and sensed exciting possibilities. We'd settled in the country—at least it seemed that way compared with Queens.

When I returned the following spring, our hundreds of trees had surrounded the house with a soaring wall of leaves. Going in and out I noticed a haunting bird sound at the end of the gravel driveway. I thought it might be a quail.

I didn't solve the quail mystery until two years later. I was home again—an unemployed college graduate living with my parents while I looked for my first job. I visited dozens of companies and mailed hundreds of résumés, but no one was hiring. With time on my hands, I sat one day in a friend's yard watching Blue Jays and chickadees take sunflower seeds from a gallon jug fashioned into a hanging bird feeder. Could I, too, lure these marvelous creatures to my yard? Maybe this could keep me busy while I waited for the economy to improve.

My first project was to build a bird feeder and birdbath; then I set up a camera to catch the parade of wings. I found a pair of World War II binoculars buried in a storage cabinet and bought Roger Tory Peterson's *Field Guide to the Birds*. With Peterson's help I identified the bird cooing at the end of the driveway: not a quail but a Mourning Dove.

It wasn't long before I outgrew backyard birding. Yearning for new birds, I set out to explore wilder places. With our dog Ms. I crawled under a fence behind our house and emerged onto the small farm of the Wakeman family. It was the beginning of my 20-year attachment to a cornfield, an apple orchard, an overgrown meadow, and a small woodland. I walked Ms. through Wakeman's Farm nearly every day, rambles that got me inextricably hooked on birds. When old age claimed my steadfast companion, I introduced a second dog, Sasha, to my private sanctuary.

In the 30 years since a friend's feeder sparked my interest in birds, I've seen a high percentage of the more than 400 species that occur in Connecticut, and for the most part I've done so within a 15-mile radius of the house on the cul-de-sac. Soon after I discovered Wakeman's Farm, I started going to Sherwood Island State Park on Long Island Sound, an oasis amid Fairfield County's built-up coastline. I made both places mine and came to know every inch of them. They were small and ordinary, but I loved them.

In time I ranged 20 minutes north to the Saugatuck Reservoir—a four-mile stretch of clear blue water surrounded by thousands of forested acres as pristine as you'll find in Connecticut. When I wasn't at Wakeman's or Sherwood Island, I was probably at the reservoir, where eagles flew, whip-poor-wills sang, and turkeys made tracks. The three places gave me a variety of habitats: coastline, farmland, inland water, and woods.

When I got my first job I moved to the bustling Saugatuck neighborhood of Westport and lived in a house that had been converted into apartments. A semester in the University of Southern California's graduate screenwriting program had intervened. I left film school with high hopes of making it big in the world of movies but found myself working in Stamford, Connecticut, as an assistant editor for a trade magazine, the "bible" of the wallpaper industry. In my next job I wrote training filmstrips for the Army.

Since 1980 I have plied the writing trade as a freelancer. When the landlord renovated my Saugatuck apartment and nearly doubled the rent, I moved to Weston, a rural suburb just north of Westport. Weston has Fairfield County's largest nature preserve and the lower half of the Saugatuck Reservoir.

My small apartment next to the garage was a writer's dream. It faced thick woods; traffic noise rarely intruded. The house, situated on two acres on a dead-end street shared with three other houses, was perched on a hill at the end of a driveway entered through stone pillars. There was a pond with snoring pickerel frogs and big fluttery goldfish, and sometimes a Great Blue Heron visited.

In eight years my elderly landlady never raised the rent. She went to the senior center nearly every day, leaving me to fantasize myself a millionaire. The fantasy ended when she moved to a condominium in Norwalk. They came from Malibu, the couple who bought the house, and I accepted their invitation to stay on at the same rent. Soon a bulldozer arrived, and for 11 months I lived on a construction site. As the renovation neared completion, the Malibu couple asked me to leave.

Now I write from an apartment in Newtown, on Fairfield County's northeast fringe. The house is on four acres next to a wooded stream with an imposing name: the south branch of the Pootatuck River. In the backyard, a dug-out section of the river forms a semicircular pond that attracts Great Blue Herons and kingfishers, muskrat and an occasional beaver, and a variable number of Mallard that in recent winters has exceeded 250. A wetlands behind the house is the remnant of a long-deserted beaver pond.

I've seen coyotes from my desk and red foxes from just outside the door. Once I glimpsed river otters—parent and youngster—loping toward the stream. At night I've heard owls—Screech-, Great Horned, and Barred—and late winter sometimes brings displaying woodcocks. When I moved here eight years ago, the forested ridge in the back was a solid black mass against the night sky. Now a few house lights flicker near the ridgetop.

Typical suburban housing lots surround me, but there are barns and woodsheds for the swallows, and a few small horse farms. A 200-acre working farm, the jewel of the neighborhood, hangs on a half mile down the road. Some people keep chickens and domesticated geese; one neighbor has peacocks that I hear on warm evenings, the human quality of their cries always bringing me to a halt.

I've all but stopped going to Sherwood Island and the Saugatuck Reservoir, because closer places have won my heart (Wakeman's Farm was long ago converted to athletic fields). My current favorite is Newtown's Upper Paugusset State Forest. I love the ups and downs of its trails, the trees that rival the biggest in all Connecticut; the Turkey Vultures, Barred Owls, Acadian Flycatchers, and Cerulean Warblers; the Wood Thrushes that in summer divvy up the forest among themselves, leaving no appropriate habitat unoccupied; the Housatonic River shoreline.

Like all the places I've adopted, the Upper Paugusset has major flaws. A logging road cuts a wide and deep gash across its center. The forest is on an unnatural stretch of the Housatonic known as Lake Lillinonah, which rises behind Shepaug Dam. Anglers leave their empty bait containers and deadly tangled lines along Pond Brook, a turbid inlet leading from a boat launch to the lake. The hiking trail passes a cove that's always filled with floating junk—tires, plastic gas cans, cut logs, Styrofoam.

That a place can be so inhospitable to wildlife yet hold my interest comes as a surprise to more demanding nature lovers. Such purists have asked why I don't pull up and move to Montana. My answer: If the mighty goshawk can live in Fairfield County, I suppose it's wild enough here for me.

Still, I don't feel entirely at home in the suburbs. The downtown streets and shops are alien to me. SUVs—a friend calls them tanks with cup holders—make me nervous. If I slow down to enjoy the scenery, it seems there's always one on my tail. After all these years, I'm still mystified by the houses I pass on my way to the woods. Some are incredibly huge. Who lives in such palaces? What do they do?

As I come around a corner along Hanover Road, another sight mystifies me: the empty parking area of the Upper Paugusset. Fairfield County has a population of close to 900,000, and these 800 acres put on one of the best nature shows around. Admission is free. So where is everybody? I'm glad, of course, to have it all to myself. We're two of a kind, this place and I—in limbo between city and country.

CHAPTER 2

TOOLS

THERE WAS ONE FEWER PERSON TO MEET THE SHOREBIRDS MIGRATING
south in the fall of 1996, one fewer pair of footprints in the marsh
mud at the mouth of the Connecticut River. Artist and field guide
author Roger Tory Peterson had died that summer at his home in
Old Lyme. At 87, the King Penguin or RTP, as admirers knew
him, was America's most renowned expert on birds.

A longtime resident of Old Lyme, Peterson put Connecticut
on the ornithological map simply by making his home here. New
Jersey has Cape May, Massachusetts has Plum Island, New York
City has Jamaica Bay, and we had Roger Tory Peterson.

In 1981 I saw him lecture to a packed auditorium at Yale
University. A tall white-haired man with chiseled features, he was an
imposing presence. He spoke with professorial dispassion, but
humor and humanity glinted through his reserve. He told of going
for an eye exam. The doctor found that Peterson had an astigmatism.

When the King Penguin asked what could be done about it, the doctor suggested he take up bird-watching.

After the lecture Peterson autographed copies of his field guide. I was too shy to approach him with mine, so I stood in the background, taking pictures. The only thing penguinish about him was his suit. With his darting eyes, aquiline nose, long fingers grasping a black-enameled pen, and unself-conscious grandeur, he was more of a benign raptor. Not entirely comfortable as the focus of a crowd of awestruck humans, he seemed inclined to fly away.

My first *Peterson's Field Guide to the Birds* was the 45th printing of his third eastern edition, published in 1947 and subtitled *Giving Field Marks of All Species Found East of the Rockies*. No one had told me that if there was one field guide to own, this was it. I came to this conclusion after walking into a bookstore, picking out a likely guide, and carrying it into the field. Of the dozen North American guides I have acquired since, I often refer to Peterson's first.

Peterson's field guide illustrations have pointers that show the distinguishing characters of each species of bird. This is the "field mark" system that he used in 1934 for the first edition of his book, published when he was 26. Earlier generations had learned about birds by "collecting" or shooting them, and by studying books laden with ornithological detail.

Peterson proved that you could learn as much, and feel better about it, by wearing binoculars and carrying his simple guide. Refined in his later guides, the field mark system, which eventually became known as the Peterson System, makes it easy to identify most birds at a glance, the way we usually see them in the field, through binoculars.

A field guide is a special breed of book, one not to be merely read. In the heat of the chase, you stop and open it. You let the mosquitoes bite until you verify a field mark. It becomes your constant companion—mine developed a permanent bend down its length from having been stuffed countless times into my back pocket. The more wear it shows, the better you like it, but once it's irretrievably lost, or damaged beyond repair, you forget sentimentality and go out and buy a new one.

My present Peterson field guide has endured many indignities. Its binding is held together by duct tape which in summer turns gooey. I have dropped it in a stream. I have found insects flattened between its pages. I sat on it repeatedly until I finally moved it from my back pocket to a belt pouch.

It has flown from the roof of my car onto the roadside. Hours later, returning to the scene of my absentmindedness, I spied the book facedown in gravel, beckoning me with its blue cover. It was a happy reunion.

A true field guide must be a bantamweight that provides instantly accessible information, so Peterson made clarity and brevity high priorities. He had the uncanny ability to extract from nature the essence of a bird and transfer it to the printed page. The color plates in his guides, reproduced from larger paintings, are free of unnecessary detail, yet they seem lifelike.

Echoing the simplicity of his painting, Peterson's vigorous field guide text tells in the fewest possible words what makes each bird unique. He calls the Long-tailed Duck "talkative," the Least Bittern "furtive," the Barn Owl "a long-legged, knock-kneed, pale, monkey-faced owl."

About the Green Heron, he noted: "When alarmed it stretches its neck, elevates a shaggy crest, and jerks its tail." The Spotted Sandpiper "teeters up and down as if a bit too delicately balanced." The Scarlet Tanager sings like "a robin with a sore throat." His writing was precise yet stylish, and he was a master of the descriptive turn of phrase. Peterson on the Brown Pelican: "Size, shape, and flight (a few flaps and a glide) indicate a pelican; the dark color and habit of plunging bill-first proclaim it this species."

Although a great believer in wildlife conservation, Peterson did not try to make people environmentally aware by railing about saving the Earth. Instead, he painted. His philosophy seems to have been that if you show people how to appreciate wildlife, they will recognize the importance of protecting it.

When I made my first tentative forays into the suburban wilderness—a Peterson field guide riding on my hip—all I wanted to know was how to tell the birds apart. Peterson told me this artistically, but there was artfulness to his method as well. The beautiful simplicity of the field mark system in a sense tricked me into learning about birds without really trying.

Today, I can identify the birds I'm likely to encounter without carrying a field guide, but if there's ever a question, I still keep Peterson's close at hand. The bent, weather-beaten, dog-eared, taped-up, unautographed field guide has earned an honored place on the front seat of my car, the only book allowed to accompany me in my pursuit of birds.

As inventor of the modern field guide—a tool that has brought so many people closer to the natural world—Peterson, in his subtle way, made a contribution to the American environmental movement that was as profound as Rachel Carson's. His eastern guide has sold millions of copies. He was working on the fifth edition the day he died. It was finished by a team of experts and published in 2002.

Peterson's bird guides are classics—and excellent choices for beginners—but they are not the last word on field identification.

Following his lead, publishers have produced high quality alternatives. First published in 1983, the *National Geographic Field Guide to the Birds of North America,* a collaborative effort of many artists and writers, represented a major departure from Peterson's approach. Not only did the National Geographic guide cover all North American species in a single, portable volume, it positioned the range maps on the same page as the bird identification illustrations and descriptions—making information more readily accessible for the birder in the field.

For a new generation interested in delving deeper into field identification, National Geographic's eagle-emblazoned guide became the one to use. The illustrations depict males, females, immatures, and seasonal plumages of many species, as well as distinct geographic races, and they usually give a hint of habitat. As in the Peterson guides, each plate shows several birds, allowing separation of species that share basic characteristics.

In 2000, artist and writer David Allen Sibley published his *Sibley Guide to Birds.* Sibley, the illustrator of *Hawks in Flight* and *A Guide to Bird-Finding in New Jersey,* had worked over the course of 12 years on the guide and its 6,600 illustrations of 810 species of North American birds.

Although heavy on artwork—the highly variable Red-tailed Hawk, for example, required some 40 paintings—in other respects the *Sibley* guide seems to follow the philosophy that less is more. Generally, it depicts only two species per page, with illustrations of each placed within a wide column, against a white background. A brief description introduces each bird, and labeled pointers show the field marks of adults (in breeding and nonbreeding plumages), juveniles, and distinguishable populations. Each column ends with a short paragraph on voice and a range map.

Sibley also peppers his roomy pages with nuances of identification that wouldn't have fit into a book of typical field guide dimensions. Few people lug the *Sibley* guide into the field—it's a reference better left at home or in the car, used to resolve identifications that elude a true field guide.

Aside from one or more of the big three identification guides, a serious birder should own guides to the occurrence and distribution of local birds. I have four such works—*Connecticut Birds*, *The Atlas of Breeding Birds of Connecticut*, *Birds of Massachusetts*, and *Bull's Birds of New York State*—and I use them almost as much as my field guides. Two other frequently used volumes in my library—*Connecticut Birding Guide* and *Finding Birds in Connecticut*—confirm Washington Irving's description of my state as one "which supplies the Union with pioneers for the mind as well as for the forest, and sends forth yearly its legions of frontier woodsmen and country schoolmasters." These books, both published in 1996, have a combined length of 1,100 pages. They cover virtually all the land in Connecticut worth birding, from parcels of a few acres to sprawling state forests. Certainly no state has been more thoroughly explored from a birder's standpoint.

A comprehensive list of region-specific ornithological references can be found in the *Birder's Catalog* of the American Birding Association, available online at www.americanbirding.org and in hard copy from the ABA sales department. The catalog includes a section on another essential tool: recordings of bird songs.

As for optics, I go cheap and ultralight, with a $150 pair of 8x40 binoculars and an old 20x spotting scope attached to a monopod. I haven't yet transferred my sighting records from notebooks to the computer, and probably never will. The thought of typing up my bird sightings at the end of the day, instead of writing them down, makes my eyelids grow heavy.

I walk in the woods at least every other day for 90 minutes or more. I almost never wear a backpack, even on long hikes. The freedom I like to feel vanishes if I'm weighed down. Anything beyond clothing is excess baggage—I want as much as possible to emulate the unencumbered body of a bird. I don't carry water unless it's very hot, and to feel truly ultralight I sometimes leave behind my binoculars.

I learned by accident the joy of walking in the wild without binoculars. I had gone to Southbury, along the east bank of the Housatonic River, in search of wintering Bald Eagles. Now, heading home, I drove over the steel bridge into Newtown. Going around a curve, I felt a thump. Some darn kid throwing a snowball, I thought.

When I got home, I couldn't find my binoculars. Then I realized they were what had made that thump. In Southbury, I had left them on the roof of the car, and they had tumbled off as I drove around the curve. How they stayed up there while I traveled a good two miles, I'll never know. I must have been quite a sight crossing the bridge and driving through town with binoculars on the roof.

I searched the roadside along the curve, but the binoculars were lost. While I shopped for a new pair—taking weeks to make a decision—I discovered how free I felt when binoculars weren't hanging around my neck like the proverbial albatross. Binoculars are essential, however, for seeing small, fast-moving birds, and I was glad to have mine with me the day I encountered the Golden-crowned Kinglet.

CHAPTER 3

A GOLDEN-CROWNED WINTER

I'M FORTUNATE TO LIVE IN A CORNER OF THE WORLD WHERE THE SEASONS are distinct and where so many birds migrate south for the winter. Between their sweetly sorrowful fall departure and their momentous spring arrival, I see what the world is like without them.

The winter landscape does have pockets of activity—well-stocked bird feeders can attract a crowd, and farms with adjacent thickets can be lively with sparrows, cardinals, finches, and crows. But most of New England's wildlands are forests that in winter support scant birdlife. The more uniform a forest's vegetation, the fewer bird species it generally has, and in winter such a place can be like a tomb. Yet the tomb forest has a beauty all its own.

On the rare day when the temperature falls to 0°F, I consider a walk in the woods obligatory. Cold profound enough to freeze the hair in your nostrils is something to experience. While celebrating one zero-degree day, I found myself in a mountain laurel thicket plucking ice from the leaves, each piece a transparent replica of the leaf it had covered, complete with venation. What could I do with such delicate, ephemeral things? I swallowed several. (Mountain laurel, I know, is toxic; the ice, it turned out, wasn't.)

Coming out of the woods that January afternoon, I heard a pair of Great Horned Owls hooting from a hemlock grove. As cold as it was, they could have already begun nesting—in Connecticut Great Horned Owls nest earlier than any other bird of prey. There were also chickadees and a Downy Woodpecker.

Chickadees, titmice, woodpeckers, nuthatches, crows, and jays are the year-round residents of southern New England's winter woods, but now and then I'll walk for miles without meeting any of them. Taking up my field notebook that evening, I'll realize I have no sightings to record. I'll search my memory, and more often than not, the day's soundtrack will hold only a peep from a chickadee, a caw from a crow.

Of the places I visit regularly in winter, the Lower Paugusset State Forest seems the most bereft of birds, especially along the Housatonic River trail section, which cuts through hemlock-covered slopes. Although the river runs deep and silent here, at the start of the trail the ear often can detect the low roar of two streams flowing down the river's steep opposite bank. Viewed through binoculars, the streams appear as mere trickles that should be hardly audible when they empty into the river, but the enveloping hills and the river's smooth surface make them resound.

That low roar, which a hiker might take for wind funneling down the river valley, is a frosty sound, like the bark of a fox or the croak of a raven. Combine it with a subfreezing temperature, a gray sky mirrored by a gray river, a trail that snakes through dark hemlock woods, and a recent snow crunching underfoot. Then you have the perfect conditions for a winter walk.

On such a day I feel wonderfully isolated, imagining myself one of the few people on Earth taking pleasure in the purity of winter. Yes, it can be lonely. One wintry afternoon I walked along the river without seeing so much as a Mallard or a Herring Gull. The woods, too, were deserted of birds.

After about 1.5 miles, the trail turns away from the river. This may be the walk's loneliest part, without the company of the water. Soon a hill covered with tall hemlocks looms up on the left; I'm well into the forest's interior. So far from roads, it's very quiet.

Prydden Brook is about ten minutes away. I usually stop at the brook and follow it down to the waterfall I call One Man's Cascade. Then I continue to the river, take a good look, and turn around. On this day I'd started late; darkness would fall long before I returned to my car. Unless I heard a Barred Owl, the most likely owl in these woods, this was looking like a walk that would go down as birdless.

Nobody knew I was there, at the edge of the universe—that's how it felt in the cold near the great Housatonic, with darkness closing in on the ancient hills and the sleeping hemlocks. While pondering my insignificance, I heard a faint pip, and with that my loneliness fell away. Suddenly I was among friends. Three high-pitched *tsees* from the hemlocks on the looming hill clinched the identification: Golden-crowned Kinglets.

Across much of the United States, Golden-crowned Kinglets are winter visitors. Most breed in Canadian spruce forests, and though some winter there as well, the vast majority move south, gathering in highest numbers in parts of the country where the temperature stays above freezing. They show up in my part of the continent in October and depart in April. A few breed in Connecticut's northwest hills, but to me the light olive kinglet is the quintessential winter bird, its constant flitting and calling one of the few signs of life in the January woods.

This species is named for the male's orange crest, which he raises in aggressive displays toward other males. Next to Ruby-throated Hummingbirds, Golden-crowned Kinglets are the smallest birds found in eastern North America. To further appreciate the four-inch-long kinglet's minuteness, compare it with the Black-capped Chickadee, a very small bird itself and one familiar to many people because it commonly visits feeders and can be found in any season. The little chickadee is 1.25 inches longer than the kinglet and weighs nearly twice as much.

At first the kinglets in the hemlocks on the looming hill were invisible. Kinglets usually feed high in conifers, moving constantly as they glean tiny insects—including scale insects, insect eggs, and dormant insect larvae—from the foliage, occasionally hovering hummingbird-like at the tips of the needles. Their high-pitched calls are hard to pinpoint, so you have to stare in the general direction of their voices until, as I like to put it, you get a level on them.

That level is the height at which they're feeding, and you won't see them until you find it. Kinglets travel in small bands, and since all members of a band often feed in the same canopy zone, you can get a level by spotting just one. If that bird disappears behind a clump of needles, or shoots to another tree, keep scanning that level and you're bound to see others.

Sometimes kinglets join foraging flocks of chickadees, titmice, and nuthatches. These half dozen were alone—feathered atoms flitting amid the hemlock spires in open defiance of winter, their nuclear energy rekindling my spirit. I didn't mind that they ignored me; kinglets may allow a close approach if they're feeding near the ground, but like other very small birds they tend to be indifferent to human proximity, tolerant rather than tame. The warmest reaction I've ever gotten from a kinglet was a blank stare.

That was in October, when kinglets have time for such a nicety. Come winter, idleness of any kind carries the risk of death. On freezing days I've never seen a Golden-crowned Kinglet perch for more than a fraction of a second. Its body temperature and metabolism are so high that it must find food every two seconds to build up the energy reserve it needs to survive the long winter night, perhaps more than doubling its store of fat over the course of a day.

What puzzles scientists is that, no matter how much a kinglet eats, apparently it cannot gather enough fuel to keep its blast furnace of a body stoked through a very cold night. To compensate for this inadequacy, the kinglet, they reason, must conserve body heat—by roosting in places insulated from the cold, such as squirrel's nests, by forming closely packed roosting groups, or by appreciably lowering its body temperature, a mechanism known as moderate nocturnal hypothermia. Whether the kinglet uses one or more of these methods has yet to be proved.

If its unremitting search for food turns up enough insects and its heat-conserving strategies (whatever they are) work, the kinglet can withstand a temperature of -40°F. Still, kinglets wintering in the most northerly latitudes suffer staggering mortality. In a severe winter storm, 100 percent of a locality's wintering population may perish.

According to Bernd Heinrich, who has studied the kinglet

in Maine, "87 percent of the population is on average normally weeded out every year." Not all kinglets succumb to winter cold. Weighed down by insulating plumage an inch thick, kinglets are poor long-distance flyers. Many of them do not survive the rigors of migration.

The kinglet bounces back from high mortality by having two broods of up to 12 young each. Many songbirds have broods less than half that size. In his book, *Winter World: The Ingenuity of Animal Survival*, Heinrich likens the kinglet's boom-and-bust life cycle to that of an annual plant.

I'm amazed that any bird survives a very cold winter night. When another winter visitor, a male Slate-colored Junco, flew into the glass of my bedroom window, I took the brief opportunity to study avian thermoregulation up close. The junco lay perfectly prone, with the tip of his bill resting on the ground. A tension in his posture suggested he was alive. I scooped him up, brought him inside, and warmed him in my cupped hands.

In his unconscious state he was a frail copy of the plump-looking juncos I see hopping around the feeder. Wondering how good a job nature had done to insulate him from the cold, I blew on his body plumage to expose his bare skin. His feathery coat parted, and I saw glimpses of the skinny, naked bird inside. The feathers were less thick than I expected—a flimsy defense against winter without muscles under the skin working to fluff them up.

I had put the junco in a towel-lined box so he could rest in a comfortable, dark place. As I was about to close it, he flew out and fluttered up against a picture window, desperate to leave my safe world of warmth. I caught him and took him outside. He zipped away when I opened my hands and, landing in a bush on a leafy hill, took a moment to get reoriented. Fluffing his feathers to trap escaping body heat and seal out the cold, he instantly regained the apparent weight of his companions at the feeder. Out here he could end up a Sharp-shinned Hawk's dinner, but this was home, and he was glad to be back.

A junco might spend a winter night in an old nest in a clump of evergreen shrubs, but the sleeping habits of Golden-crowned Kinglets have thus far escaped the notice of ornithologists. One kinglet was seen entering a leafy squirrel's nest at dusk, and a student of Bernd Heinrich flushed one before dawn from a brush pile topped with snow.

Neither observation was definitive. After getting details of the very brief sighting at the squirrel's nest, Heinrich was skeptical, and I wish his student had seen the kinglets enter the brush pile at dusk and remain there until after dark. Flushing the kinglets before dawn strongly suggests they spent the night, but it's possible they roosted elsewhere and moved to the brush pile before the student happened by.

The kinglet is common, with a range that encompasses most of North America. I'm sure someone, somewhere on this continent, has happened upon roosting kinglets. Maybe scores of people have. Their observations just haven't found their way into the scientific literature.

I returned to the Lower Paugusset State Forest late one January day to solve this mystery for myself. It was after a heavy rain—28°F, cloudy, calm, and livelier than I expected. Along with chickadees and the other usual birds, I heard a Northern Flicker, a Pileated and a Red-bellied Woodpecker, and a Winter Wren. Hearing a *tsee* early on, I thought I'd found kinglets, but it turned out to be the very similar call of a Brown Creeper.

At the looming hill, which I'll always associate with kinglets, I searched the hemlocks in vain. My luck changed at my turnaround point, swollen Prydden Brook, where kinglet calls rose above the noise of swift water. This was good timing: 4:30, just as darkness was settling in. I couldn't see them, but the kinglets seemed to be calling from the very tops of hemlocks lining the brook—too high a roosting place for my taste, but that's where the foliage is thickest.

There was unusual urgency in their voices. Could this be a special cry that rallies them to a communal roost? With the posing of that question, my investigation ended, because I let the cascade lure me away. The walk there takes a minute, and the previous day's heavy rain promised a good show. Just a quick look, I told myself. But the cascade flowed so forcefully that I took extra time. When I got back to where the kinglets had been, I heard no calls, and it was too dark to look elsewhere. The case of the roosting kinglet would have to wait.

The winter of 2003 spat in the face of global warming. That January was the coldest I could remember. Subfreezing temperatures persisted for two weeks, and overnight lows sometimes hovered around 0°F. One morning, when it was -1°F, the leaves of the rhododendron outside the door were curled as tightly as cigarettes, but, incredibly, the pond wasn't completely frozen. With their paddling feet, the Mallard had saved themselves a crescent-shape sliver of open water.

I'd been filling the feeders and throwing down seed late at night so the birds could wake to an easy meal. Back inside, I'd burrow under four blankets and maybe get up in the middle of the night to turn up the heat. Would the birds make it? I've always worried too much about their winter survival. Ironically, the ferocity of January '03 partly cured me of that by forcing me to look more closely at their remarkable adaptations to cold weather. I've learned that empathy for the birds can be taken too far.

In *The Outermost House*, Henry Beston writes, "The animal shall not be measured by man. In a world older and more complete than ours they move finished and complete, gifted with extensions of the senses we have lost or never attained, living by voices we shall never hear." It is, in part, a warning against excessive anthropomorphizing of birds and other animals. In my case, I've erred when I consider the plight of birds in winter by putting myself in their place—by thinking it's a feathered me out there in the frigid darkness. I'm perched on a branch, huddled against the trunk of an old evergreen, unable to hide from the howling wind.

But this picture is all wrong. The birds at the feeder have evolved for life in this chilly part of the world. This is not really where I belong, however. My human origins can be traced to Africa. Essentially, I'm a transplanted equatorial primate. No wonder this long spell of polar days is getting me down.

I'm not suggesting, and I'm sure neither is Beston, that we let the pendulum swing to the opposite extreme and reject all commonality with birds. I have no patience for people who believe intelligence, memory, emotion, and the capacity to feel cold and pain cannot exist in nonhuman animals. That animals do possess these attributes should be self-evident to all of us. Yet lack of empathy for other animals, one of the most inhumane of human traits, is disturbingly common.

Excessive anthropomorphism is also common, and though not as dangerous, it's distasteful because it, too, denies animals their identity. By imagining myself a roosting chickadee, I'm imposing my needs on his. The chickadee, however, does not miss my relatively airtight home, my warm bed, my roaring furnace, and my hot food. A freezing night without these things is inconceivable to me, but to him it's perfectly natural. My human conceit resists the notion that a small bird can endure winter's unbridled fury, but covered from head to tail with nature's best insulating material, even the least hardy species has winter protection superior to that of the best equipped mountaineer.

Sleeping birds normally fluff their body plumage, tuck their heads into their shoulder feathers, and shiver to stay warm. Their tough, usually unfeathered legs and feet have circulatory adaptations that minimize heat loss. Many resting birds balance on one leg and warm the other leg by pulling it into their belly feathers. When it gets as cold as it was that January, birds may take one or more additional steps to conserve heat: finding a warmer roost (some tunnel into the snow), sleeping in groups, inducing moderate nocturnal hypothermia.

At the feeder they press their fluffed underparts against their feet, and in near-zero weather they eat frantically, as they do early in a snowstorm, when ground birds in particular seem to know that seeds may be hard to find later. If a high wind kicks up, my feeder birds point their heads directly into the blast and lower their bodies, presenting a streamlined contour that makes them less subject to buffeting.

Beston admires the sensory powers of birds; the power to survive a harsh winter is among their other gifts. The chickadee I watch from behind my glass door doesn't need my pity. This bird is a pro at outdoor winter living, and with a year-round range that extends into Alaska, it probably doesn't find a cold spell in Connecticut very challenging.

Carolina Wrens, near the northern edge of their range here, are weather weaklings compared with chickadees. They forage mainly for insects in brushy, leaf-littered habitat, and after deep, persisting snow, a population is likely to crash. Where January temperatures stay consistently below 19°F, Carolina Wrens do not usually become established.

Looking at the one that's been coming to my feeder for two weeks, you wouldn't suspect it faced a life-threatening situation. It feeds with an almost casual air, seems very picky (atypically preferring millet and sunflower seed to suet), and never stays long. I'd like to think I'm helping pull it through the winter, but it must be finding the bulk of its food elsewhere—either in the understory and hedges on the other side of the house, where I've heard a Carolina Wren sing during warm months, or at another feeder with better pickings. It may be that snow, of which there isn't much, is a bigger problem for the Carolina Wren than cold.

The wren's matter-of-factness inspires me. Reports of the crushing cold are all over the news, and this bird—reputedly so vulnerable—goes about its business as if nothing's wrong. It accepts what it can't change. Maybe it won't survive the winter, but it never surrenders. On the coldest days the wren visits, the titmouse sings, the mallard bathes and quarrels, and the flicker happily probes a snowless bit of sun-warmed grass next to the driveway.

In the sunlight of late January, I can already detect the nascent glow of summer. The world is half an hour less dark than it was a month ago. But something else has been lighting up my winter days.

At 5:09 p.m. on January 21, 2003, while walking the logging road of the Upper Paugusset State Forest, I solved the mystery of the roosting Golden-crowned Kinglet—to my satisfaction, if not to the satisfaction of science. I was coming down a hill near the road's western end and had just passed the intersection with the white trail. I turned around to look for a kinglet calling from high in the deciduous trees overhanging the road but couldn't get a level on it.

Then the kinglet dropped into view and came to the ground. It landed about 25 feet away, next to a grass- and fern-covered mound of tree roots jutting from the shoulder of the road. It was a male, and he called a couple of times before entering a narrow, shallow crevice between the edge of the mound and the surrounding snow. In a moment he came out, called one last time, and went back in. I never saw him leave.

That was about 13 minutes after sunset. I waited, my eyes locked on the crevice except for the few times I checked my watch. By 5:30 it was fairly dark, and I figured the kinglet was in for the night. I noticed stars at 5:40; at 5:41 a Barred Owl let out a single hoot. I left at 5:45, when it was quite dark, stepping lightly on the icy snow but making a good deal of noise anyway.

I planned to get up very early the next morning to catch the kinglet leaving his roost. Between nervously anticipating the 5 a.m. alarm, and worrying about the kinglet in his icy ditch of a bedroom (bad old anthropomorphic habits die hard), I stayed awake all night. At the appointed hour I forced myself into motion and dressed in twos—two sweatshirts, two hats, two pairs of pants and gloves.

It was 7°F and still dark when, at 6:22 a.m., I reached my observation post of the previous evening, some 25 feet from the roost. I spent most of the 52 minutes until sunrise congratulating myself for dressing warmly enough to stand still in the inhuman cold. I also passed time by keeping track of awakening birds. Crows were up first, calling at 6:50. A goldfinch started in about five minutes later; then came a nuthatch, a Blue Jay, a Red-bellied Woodpecker, and maybe a bluebird.

I waited two hours but never saw the kinglet emerge. If he had, it would be irrefutable proof of roosting, but I saw all the evidence I needed the previous evening. Overnight, something must have forced him out. Birds get rousted from sleep often enough—while putting out seed the other night, I inadvertently flushed a flock of waxwing-size birds from a red cedar. During the long winter night, many animals travel the logging road. A deer or a coyote walking by the kinglet roadhouse may have prompted its occupant to seek more secure quarters.

Less likely outcomes: The kinglet died from the cold, or a predator caught him. There was also the remote possibility that he was still in there, so before I left at 8:20 I marched to the mound, pished and talked loudly, and gently drew a long stick across the crevice edges. Curtained by grass and ferns hanging from the mound, and with a tapering shelf of snow projecting into it from below, the two-inch-deep crevice offered good camouflage and a measure of insulation from the night chill.

The kinglet could have crawled under dead leaves lining the crevice to get farther away from the cold. A more scientifically inclined investigator would have dug around for physical evidence of roosting—droppings, down, or a dead kinglet—and broken away the snow shelf to see the full extent of the crevice. I declined to destroy the roost lest the kinglet should return.

My one concession to science was to photograph the mound. I went back late in the day, so I could get the sun shining on it, and shot it from every angle. Then I waited for the kinglet. I still had questions: Kinglets are gregarious by day, so why was he roosting alone? Where were his companions, and how did he reunite with them? When he woke, prepared to forage without pause for ten hours, where did he go first?

I may never know the answers. The kinglet didn't come. It could be that he used a different roost every night, one near wherever he happened to be foraging when darkness fell. I wasn't disappointed. I had no right to be. He'd given me a great gift.

CHAPTER 4

WARBLERS

EVERY SPRING THE BIRD POPULATION IN NORTH AMERICA GROWS BY TWO billion to five billion with the arrival of neotropical migrants—birds that winter in Mexico, Central America, South America, and the West Indies. In parts of the United States and Canada, neotropical migrants constitute more than 50 percent of nesting species. They may depart soon after raising their broods, some beginning their southward journeys in August.

Neotrops, as they are sometimes called, enhance the newly green spring landscape with their often brilliant colors and beautiful songs. They include familiar species like the shade tree-loving Baltimore Oriole, striking forest denizens like the Scarlet Tanager, aerialists like the Barn Swallow, flycatchers like the Eastern Kingbird, and virtuoso singers like the Wood Thrush.

The wood-warblers—members of the family Parulidae—form a very large group of neotrops. Of the 115 wood-warbler species in this strictly New World family, about 60 range north of Mexico. Unless I see at least 30 of them in May, when their numbers peak, I feel I haven't paid fitting tribute to the spring migration.

Drawn north that month as if by a magnet, these energized little bundles of yellow and green blow through the trees, singing constantly. No songbirds evince the power, beauty, and mystery of migration more spectacularly than the warblers. Following an ancient migratory urge, they reappear as the trees leaf out, feeding on insects. Some remain to breed, others go farther north.

Migrating warblers do most of their traveling at night. In the morning they seem to favor migratory funnels—coastal woods, river valleys, and ridges—where they forage among the leaves to refuel for the next leg of their journey. On a good day, in a few hours a birder may see 15 to 20 of the more than 30 species of warblers regularly found in eastern North America. Warblers also occur in the West, but the diversity of species that breed north of Mexico is richer in the East.

The migration of warblers through many of the northern states usually peaks during the second and third weeks of May, their numbers on a given day largely determined by the weather. Birders have all kinds of meteorological nostrums for predicting the days that will bring big flights of migrants, and for years I was among them. In May I would become preoccupied with weather reports. When all the signs suggested that a mass warbler movement was imminent, I went to bed thinking, tomorrow's the day!

Most often I was disappointed. Ultimately I had to accept the fact that there was little correlation between my migration theories and what the warblers were doing. These days, like the warblers, I follow my instincts: I go birding if it feels right.

My time in the field seems to confirm that habitat destruction in breeding, wintering, and migration-stopover areas is reducing the eastern songbird population. When I began birding, there were more than a few days in May when warblers poured through the woods. The overlapping songs of all the different species confused yet delighted me. Now such days are rare. I can still see 30 species by month's end, but few species occur in large numbers.

The more common warblers—parula, Yellow-rumped, and some eight other species—are easy to find, and I quickly add the widespread breeders to my list: Yellow Warbler, Black-and-white, Worm-eating, Ovenbird, and Yellowthroat. The Hooded Warbler is one of the less common breeders, but every year I meet a few. Pine warblers, Prairies, and Louisiana Waterthrushes can be relied upon to appear in their respective habitats.

Cape May and Tennessee Warblers are usually scarce, but in some years, at particular locations, they can be fairly common, though they tend not to linger. Certain warblers seem to travel singly and move through quickly, providing only a narrow window of opportunity. In my area, the Northern Waterthrush usually falls into this category. Nashville, Blackburnian, and Wilson's Warblers are not rare, but they can be somewhat elusive. Palm Warblers come early in the season, weeks before Bay-breasteds and Blackpolls, whose appearance indicates that the migration is winding down.

If I bird consistently, by mid-May I might already have seen or heard 27 species without undue effort, but 30 is the magic number, and to hit it I will need at least three genuine rarities. A Prothonotary Warbler or a Kentucky could pop up on our birding hotline, the Connecticut Rare Bird Alert. I could wait until late May and maybe find a Mourning Warbler or a Yellow-breasted Chat. Casting my fate literally to the wind, however, is risky birding business. To be assured of 30 warblers in May, I must make a pilgrimage to Connecticut's warbler mecca: River Road in Kent.

This dead-end dirt road follows a peaceful stretch of the Housatonic River and connects to the Appalachian Trail. There are more-famous warbler hot spots—Cape May, New Jersey; Point Pelee, Ontario; Mount Auburn Cemetery in Cambridge, Massachusetts; New York's Central Park; and, earlier in the season, High Island on the Texas coast. But River Road will do. It's close, fairly wild, and very beautiful—and it should put me over the top. In spring its woods and brushy clearings come alive with songbirds, including certain warbler specialties.

Along River Road, Cerulean Warblers, rare elsewhere in the state, are virtually guaranteed. For several years running, I joined other birders in watching the very rare Yellow-throated Warbler, a species that normally ranges no farther north than Pennsylvania, sing from the top of a massive streamside sycamore. The Golden-winged Warbler, yet another rarity, can sometimes be found in overgrown fields along the trail, betraying itself with its buzzy song.

There is also a chance of coming upon a riotous migration party—bands of warblers passing through. When I find a warbler party in progress, I stand under their trees and watch. Fluttering through the twigs in flocks of mixed species, gleaning insects from the budding leaves, they seem indifferent to uninvited guests like me. The diminutive warblers live a hyperactive existence on a different plane. They are absorbed in their journeys; I am but a ponderous earthbound primate. They pass above me in waves, submerging me in song.

Sooner or later even warblers must come down to earth. Some species spend the most vulnerable period of their lives on the ground, a fact brought home to me on the hiking trail that runs along the west side of the Saugatuck Reservoir. I suppose I've hiked sections of this trail a thousand times, but the odd sensation that brought my gaze to my feet one summer afternoon was something new.

A Worm-eating Warbler had flapped across my path, grazing my boot with its wings. Now it was fluttering along the forest floor and chipping nervously, behavior that meant it probably had a nest nearby. Worm-eating Warblers nest on the ground, and they defend their eggs or young by trying to lure predators away.

Although tempted to search for the nest, I gave the area only a cursory look. Even with a good clue like this, nest finding requires patience. I wanted to get back into the rhythm of walking, and let the warbler, probably an incubating female, get back to her eggs.

Returning along this stretch of trail a half hour later, I had forgotten the warbler, until she cut me off again. She squeezed under my right boot just before it hit the ground. This time I concentrated on where she first appeared and found the nest almost immediately. It was tucked into the side of a leafy knoll, just two feet off the trail.

Next to a rock, and overhung with a shelf of fallen leaves, the nest contained four tiny whitish eggs flecked with brown. Although I had never found a Worm-eating Warbler nest, I quickly moved on. Every second I lingered exposed the eggs to danger and kept the female from incubating. I was careful not to touch the nest. It would have been a death sentence for the eggs, because the scent of a human, often leading to food, attracts predators.

Even my innocent pause put a worrisome glitch in my scent trail. Hours later, a rapacious raccoon foraging in the darkness might know I had stopped. Its suspicions aroused, it could start sniffing around and find the nest. As I headed back to the car, I wondered how Worm-eating Warblers survive when they build their nests on the ground, so vulnerable to predators. Walking the same trail a few days later, I had trouble finding the nest, though I had taken note of nearby landmarks. The problem was, I was still looking for the whitish eggs. Soon I realized that where the eggs had been, there were now four nestlings. Covered in brownish-gray down, they blended into the shadow of the overhanging leaves. The baby birds huddled together, quiet and motionless. The mother flew off as usual but seemed no more agitated than she had been when guarding the eggs. I kept this visit even briefer than the first.

More than a week had passed by the time I checked the warblers again. The nest was empty and intact, and I was relieved to find no signs of disaster: blood, feathers, or other remains. Surely a raiding raccoon would have dislodged the fine grasslike stems resting on the nest's front rim. One thing did bother me: the silence. If the nestlings fledged, where had they gone?

A few minutes' walk from the nest, just as I was accepting the worst, I flushed a juvenile Worm-eating Warbler from the side of the trail. Flapping furiously but moving slowly, it rose into the air and made a precarious landing in a sapling a few feet away. An adult then flew in quickly and gracefully, chipping at me in anger. Stubby-tailed and plump-looking, the young bird was mostly pale yellow, its crown showing just a hint of the bold dark stripes that distinguish the adult. Consistent with my policy of noninterference, I kept going. On my return I saw two young birds and an adult.

Unlike the open deciduous woods around the nest, this rocky slope offered plenty of cover. At the approach of danger, the awkward-flying young had mountain laurel thickets and a spattering of hemlocks in which to hide. I can't prove these warblers were from the nest I had found, but I believe they were. The young were the right age, and on subsequent walks I would see a family of three or more Worm-eating Warblers within a hundred yards of the nest.

They were lucky birds, I thought, but on reflection I realized this was underestimating them. Like the thief in Edgar Allan Poe's "Purloined Letter," the adult female I had almost stepped on was a master of the art of deception. She had placed her well-camouflaged nest "immediately beneath the nose of the whole world, by way of best preventing any portion of that world from perceiving it"—a survival strategy that protected her eggs through 13 days of incubation, and her nestlings until they fledged 10 days later.

As good as this survival strategy is, we can greatly increase its effectiveness by observing a simple rule: Stay on the hiking trail, especially in spring and summer, and if a dog comes along on such outings, never let it off the leash. Roaming dogs wreak havoc in the suburban wilderness. A dog galloping through the woods at 25 miles an hour has a great time, but think of the cost: It destroys plant and insect life, terrifies any animal it flushes, and tears up the terrain. With a single footfall, a dog can trample to death an entire brood of ground-nesting birds or small mammals.

How birds persist when they are stalked by this and a hundred other dangers always amazes me. Many species are in trouble, it's true. I don't let that stop me from exulting in the success of those that, like the Worm-eating Warbler, manage to beat the odds.

In that spirit I sought out a warbler that had wandered from the Far West to the Connecticut coast. I learned of its arrival from the rare bird alert. I don't usually chase after staked-out birds, but I had business in Greenwich and would be driving past Byram Park, where this extraordinary rarity, a Black-throated Gray Warbler, had been seen on and off for a few days. On I-95, I passed a car with birding decals on the windows and knew where its occupant, coffee cup in hand, was headed.

After correcting a wrong turn, I arrived to find this birder scanning the reddish rock outcropping near the park exit. We walked along the rock face, checking every bird. It was a lively spot, with White-throated Sparrows darting among the shrubs, rustling in the leaves, making their thin call, and occasionally breaking into song. A Carolina Wren chimed in and its small cousin, a Winter Wren, briefly emerged from a bush. I raised my binoculars to every bird that showed itself, but most often found myself looking at House Sparrows or House Finches. Still, there was plenty of action: a Ruby-crowned Kinglet popped up; chickadees and titmice filtered in and out of the treetops; cardinals chipped and a mockingbird chacked; Blue Jays and crows scoffed at the morning chill with raucous voices. My heart quickened when I spied a warbler, a Nashville—ordinarily a satisfying sighting, but not the prize I wanted.

An hour after we started searching, the other birder and I stood at one end of the rock outcropping. At the opposite end, another pair of birders was focused on some weeds. We heard one of them say, "Here it is," and we ran to join them.

The Black-throated Gray Warbler foraged before us in the grass, oblivious to our gawking. Had it been here all along, or had it just flown into the area? The pleasure of viewing this striking rarity instantly eclipsed such questions. People driving through the park would never guess that our group of transfixed binocular holders was communing with a feathered soul that normally doesn't venture east of Colorado.

According to the state's official bird checklist, the Black-throated Gray Warbler has been seen in Connecticut fewer than five times in this century. Ornithologists call such a rarity an "accidental vagrant," a description that hardly reflects the heroic odyssey of this little wanderer. This five-inch bird, weighing no more than a few coins, in all likelihood scaled our mightiest mountain range and voyaged across treeless plains inhospitable to perching birds, traversing perhaps 3,000 miles of unfamiliar terrain. It must have endured storms, evaded hawks, surmounted human obstacles, and known true isolation in darkest night. Here it settled, on the shore of Long Island Sound, creating a stir among birders—more lost than I could imagine. But this is a human's view. The warbler hadn't read the field guides that say it should be there and not here. All nature is its home. It sees the same moon and stars here as in California, finds similar insect food, associates with some of the same species, rides the same wind. It may not have felt lost or noticed the absence of others of its kind. Still, its migratory compass was probably out of alignment. Would it perish when winter arrived? Or would instinct then guide it to milder climes?

We watched the warbler fly to the other end of the rock, but soon it returned, flitting along the ground and rising to the top of the ledge. It moved among weeds, shrubs, and trees. The temperature seemed barely above freezing, but the rock, facing southeast, received the sun and radiated its warmth enough to stir insects, and we saw the warbler snap up a fly.

The warbler had a black cap and ear patch, a conspicuous white stripe over the eye, flanks streaked with black, and a yellow spot between the eye and bill. A few fine black brush strokes painted its gray back, the constantly flitting tail showed flashes of white, and a narrow black wedge crossed the top of its white breast.

Although the bird was boldly patterned, its throat appeared pale, not black. Adult male Black-throated Grays have a black throat in spring; in fall, the tips of the newly molted throat feathers are edged in white. The white throats of some females become mottled with black in spring, but all female plumages are rather dull overall, so this was probably an immature male. His call was like a Myrtle Warbler's—a rough-edged note, but shorter and softer. The rock's vegetation teemed with birds and its flat surface amplified their sounds, but the Black-throated Gray did not join the others, and his faint chip was sometimes lost amid their calls. This seemed perfectly fine for him—his sprightly actions radiated happiness.

Feeling a chill, I hoped he would turn south or somehow find his way back to the other side of the Rocky Mountains.

CHAPTER 5

THE GOSHAWK

FOR EARLY SUMMER, IT WAS A COOL DAY. I DROVE TO A HIKING TRAIL IN
northern Fairfield County—never mind exactly where. When I
got out of the car I felt cold, even in a vest and long-sleeved shirt.
A few days earlier, a Pine Warbler sang at a pond near the trailhead, but not today. Following the rugged trail along the hemlock-
covered ridge, I forgot the cold and listened for other birds.

From the woods sloping above me, I heard a thrush. The song
was distant and faint. I thought it was a Wood Thrush until I
stopped and, concentrating, heard the distinctive keynote and
ethereal strains of a Hermit Thrush. Like the Pine Warbler, the
Hermit Thrush is an uncommon nesting bird for southwestern
Connecticut, where it keeps to cool, coniferous woods resembling
territory farther north.

I walked the rest of the trail thinking how pleasant it was to
have the Hermit Thrush for a summer neighbor. On the way back

I stopped and listened for it again. This time the song sounded much closer; I could distinguish even its highest notes. Yet occasionally the thrush sounded far away, and I wondered if I was hearing two birds.

Another sound distracted me as I approached a stream—a single emphatic note like the first note of an Acadian Flycatcher's two-note song. An Acadian Flycatcher would be another unusual find, so I strayed from the trail, hoping to glimpse it and hear it break into full song. Each time I went toward the sound, the bird moved away. Although at times it was as close as 20 feet, under the light-blocking hemlocks I never saw it. The bird tired of this hide-and-seek and became silent. I returned to the trail unable to confirm my hunch. Whatever it was, this bird didn't want to be seen.

Ahead, Blue Jays were in an uproar. Perhaps they were screaming at a crow, but on this overcast day I hoped for an owl. I headed uphill to the commotion and could see the jays moving about, the cause of their distress hidden by lush foliage. I was relying on the cacophony to mask the leaves and sticks crunching under my feet, but the mystery bird detected me. A large, dark form flew to another tree with the jays in pursuit.

I steered toward the noisy jays and stared at the section of canopy they encircled. After a few more steps I froze to the piercing cry—*klee, klee, klee, klee!*—of a Northern Goshawk. Finally, my eyes caught a large bird of prey spreading two broad, stiff wings. But it was not preparing to escape. This bird's object was attack.

The goshawk dropped from its perch and shot straight at me, somehow streaking through the trees without stirring a branch. Its battle cry crescendoed as it veered off only feet from my head, landing on a branch that gave me an unobstructed view. I focused my binoculars on this imposing hawk, the incarnation of wildness. The goshawk has reason to feel bold. It is the largest accipiter, a genus of hawks adapted for life in the woods. With stocky wings and a long tail, the goshawk can maneuver through the trees at high speed, accelerating quickly and turning sharply in pursuit of explosive grouse and nimble squirrels.

When not broadcasting its presence with alarm calls, the goshawk patiently waits in a tree until spurred into action by the movement of a prey animal, or it patrols the woodland corridors swiftly and almost silently, in either case often surprising its victims. The red squirrel that becomes a goshawk's meal may not have seen or heard it coming. If a prey animal flees, the mighty goshawk can overtake and seize it. So highly evolved is the goshawk that, if sufficient prey is available, and if this consummate killer is hungry enough, it can take victims seemingly at will.

Among the accipiters, females are larger than males. The robust bird filling the glass of my binoculars was undoubtedly a female. She bristled with wild energy, glaring at me with orange eyes made fiercer by a broad white eyebrow stripe. Now and then she flinched. The Blue Jays still dove at her, behavior known as mobbing. Small birds often mob larger ones that pose a threat. Hawks, owls, and nest robbers such as crows are the most frequent targets. Jays themselves are mobbed by other birds because, like the crow, they steal eggs and prey on nestlings. By mobbing the goshawk, the jays alert one another to the danger and may even drive the killer off.

Built powerfully and cloaked in silvery gray—with a dark cap, fine light gray breast barring, broad shoulders, and bushy white undertail coverts—the goshawk stood in high relief against the looming forest. Few animals wear their wildness so well.

The goshawk could have been better named. "Gos" is Old English for "goose"—not the hawk's usual prey. Its Latin name, however, speaks the truth: *Accipiter gentilis* is hawk nobility. Also known as the Dove Hawk, the goshawk inhabits boreal and temperate forests of North America and Eurasia; in the United States, it breeds most commonly in the Northeast, in mountains of the West, and around the Great Lakes. Formerly, it occurred regularly in summer only in the most northern states and in mountainous areas farther south.

Over recent decades its southern range has expanded in response to reforestation and to laws that protect raptors, among other migratory birds. Now the goshawk nests in much of southern New England. In my state it lives not only in the countrified Litchfield Hills, but also in recesses of the more wooded suburbs, where it enjoys insulation from people—except for occasional run-ins with hikers and birders, who need the woods almost as much as the goshawk does.

Klee, klee, klee, klee!—she came at me again. I ducked reflexively as this formidable raptor with a wingspan approaching four feet swooped down on me at, by my estimate, 30 miles an hour. When she veered away, I had to admire her courage. Without hesitation, she challenged an intruder more than three times her height. I admired the audacious pack of Blue Jays, too. Goshawks are deft killers capable of snatching a Blue Jay out of the air, but this one had lost the crucial element of surprise.

Where they nest, goshawks boldly attack human trespassers. In Connecticut they lay their eggs in April. The eggs hatch in May, and in early summer one to three young may be fledging. This female was probably guarding a young goshawk nearby. Perhaps the unseen father was preparing to join the battle.

A human being's large size and vertical stance do not deter the goshawk. Neither does a hiker's innocence. That I meant no harm was irrelevant. As a member of a predatory species, I had to be challenged.

The female's call signaled another attack. To spare the family further anxiety, and avoid provoking the wrath of the male, I withdrew. I must have crossed the perimeter of the defended area, because the attack never came.

I was elated when I reached my car. I'd found a rare nesting goshawk and faced nature at its wildest. I turned up the stereo on the way home. I passed a runner and a cyclist but fought off the urge to stop and tell them about the goshawk.

On the same trail one year later, a pair of Northern Goshawks had me pinned to the ground. I have no doubt it was the same female aided by her faithful mate. The instant they detected my intrusion, their alarm calls rang out, and from a thickly wooded slope they burst into view.

In seconds these feathered stealth fighters separated and stationed themselves in low hemlock branches, with me in the middle. Now they had me in their crosshairs and were taking turns launching themselves at me. Their loud cries of protest never let up.

As the goshawks streaked toward me, voices rising, I felt sure they would strike, but at the last moment they swerved up and away. In a defensive crouch, I pulled down my hat brim to shield my eyes from their menacing talons, and each time they passed I raised a hand to keep them from raking my head. I was waiting for my chance to bolt.

They shot at me repeatedly through the densely packed hemlocks, skillfully avoiding all woody obstacles. After buzzing me, they would sweep up to a perch and turn to face me. For such large birds, their quickness was remarkable. While they got set for another launch, I stole some close looks. They would take several seconds to reach me, I estimated—a few flaps to gain speed, then a glide. My calculation was way off. They were on me an instant after launching.

They flew close to the ground, like radar-evading bombers, using the hiking trail as a flight path. The trail, overhung with hemlock branches, formed a dim forest tunnel. They sped through it and locked onto me, eyes filled with rage. They attacked with head and wings aligned in a glide. Their head-on approach made them hard to see, like paper turned edgewise, and I could not accurately judge their distance.

Their unbelievable speed and virtual imperceptibility left me helpless to gauge the precise moment to protect myself. They overwhelmed me with air superiority. The goshawks seemed to possess superavian power.

Finally I saw my opening. When both goshawks were perched at the inward end of the trail, I broke away, running for the trailhead without looking back. I ran as hard as I could, but I wasn't really afraid. I ran with the thrill of having faced primeval wildness.

More than ten years since these encounters, goshawks still nest along this ridge. It could be the same pair, because the life span of this species can exceed 11 years. I took a friend to see them last April. When we entered the territory of the nest, a female came to meet us.

She advanced and retreated half a dozen times as we tried to get a good look. She watched us continuously and called loudly, but she kept her distance—goshawks are less aggressive toward a group of people than toward a single intruder. My friend felt sorry about disturbing her, so we left after a few minutes.

Females begin to molt before laying eggs, which may explain why this one had some missing wing feathers. The molt is a time of high stress for birds, but the goshawk pair had another problem: On the way out we noticed a large nest only yards from the trail. A breeding territory can contain up to eight nests. By switching among them from year to year, the pair may lessen the risk of parasites and disease. Studies in eastern forests suggest that goshawks prefer nesting near trails, which may serve as flight corridors.

If the nest beside the trail was the active one, hikers would pass very closely. I wasn't too concerned, however. Few hikers know about the trail, and because it's remote, steep, and dark, even fewer use it. We weren't about to return any time soon, so the pair might just succeed in raising a new generation.

I've found goshawks nesting in another Fairfield County location. To protect the pair's anonymity, I'll only say that they live somewhere along the Housatonic River. A Turkey Vulture helped lead me to their nest on a blustery April day.

As I hiked up a hill through a hemlock stand, the vulture soared just above the canopy. A female goshawk's bulky form rocketed toward it. The goshawk called aggressively and buzzed the vulture three times. I heard a great rush of wings but could not tell whether there was physical contact.

The goshawk drove the vulture away and flew toward the river. I lost sight of her but followed her direction in the hope of finding the nest. I checked only deciduous trees, since goshawks in eastern forests tend not to nest in hemlocks. When the river came into view, there was an unmolested Turkey Vulture quartering above the bank. The understory gave way to expanses of leafy ground. It was a park-like setting amid the deep woods, and I envied the goshawks their home.

Although I ignored the hemlocks, there were too many trees to search. I changed my tactics: I was, you might say, feeling my way to the goshawk's nest. A rapid succession of high-pitched clucks seemed to come from a tall, skinny black birch. My eyes followed the unfamiliar sound up the trunk. A large stick nest sat in a crotch about 45 feet above the ground, 25 feet from the treetop.

The loosely constructed nest looked at least three feet wide across the top. The sticks were of uniform diameter, with no green sprigs. It was definitely a goshawk's nest, but it seemed unfinished. After several long looks through my binoculars, I realized it was occupied. The female's long, rounded tail extended beyond the rim.

When I noticed her, I left. She had showed no reaction— except for the clucking, if indeed she had produced it—and though she stayed perfectly still while I trudged up to the tree and stared at her home, she must have been in an extreme state of alarm. Later, I learned why she hadn't attacked. This was the one time a human being can enter the domain of nesting goshawks without feeling their wrath. "During incubation, males are secretive and females rarely flush to defend the site even when intruders are directly below the nest," say John R. Squires and Richard T. Reynolds in their goshawk monograph for *The Birds of North America.*

This behavior usually continues after hatching, until the nestlings are at least nine days old. Were the female to leave the nest too frequently during the early stages of development, she would subject her eggs and young nestlings to potentially fatal cold. Females have been observed to take a break of up to ten minutes after four hours of incubating. The male, who supplies the female with prey from courtship through the early nestling period, may sit in while the female feeds. This female may have been on a feeding break when she buzzed the Turkey Vulture.

Young goshawks become independent when they are 65 to 95 days old, the larger females needing more time than males. By midsummer, some juveniles have already acquired the powers of their parents. One such bird, a female, confronted me in July at the site where I had seen her father in March. She flew out of nowhere and landed with a thud in a tree 35 feet away.

She scolded me with nasal calls, then departed as mysteriously as she had arrived. With astonishing speed and agility, she dove behind a knoll. Because I didn't see her rise, I thought she might have killed a chipmunk. When I got to the other side of the knoll she was gone. Apparently she shot away while hugging the ground. If she were an older, more territorial female, I would have suspected she was toying with me—objecting noisily at my approach and pretending to escape, only to wait awhile and come up silently from behind to teach me a lesson.

The Housatonic River female is sneaky like that. A year before discovering her nest, I was crossing her territory on the hiking trail. She flew out screaming from the hemlock stand and rushed me. I hit the ground, smacking my knee into a rock.

Next she came at me from the other direction. I raised my hands and she veered away, farther from me than she had the first time, as if respectful of a human's natural weaponry. She had incredibly fast reflexes. She put on the brakes and swerved the instant I tried to defend myself.

When she retreated and moved about the canopy unthreateningly, I thought she had finally relaxed. She seemed to realize I was just passing through, so I relaxed as well and continued walking. I followed the trail through the hemlock stand. At the top of the hill I would be safe.

A glance over my shoulder made me rethink the situation. Gray wings stretched across my field of vision. One of the world's fiercest predators was hurtling up the trail toward my head. I dropped down so fast I snapped my neck. The goshawk passed over me. Then I ran.

She had been stalking me the whole time. Goshawks are powerful hunters, gray ghosts able to disappear into the forest, merge with it. They're so fast your eyes can hardly follow them. They can detect you from hundreds of yards away although you may be walking softly, obscured by dense evergreens. If you see them it's only because they're permitting it. If they want to surprise you there's little you can do to prevent it.

Goshawks prey heavily on birds—in my locale they seem to have a taste for crows and for Rock Doves, or pigeons. On walks along the Housatonic, I have come across a number of butchering logs where goshawks pluck and devour their victims. Usually all that remains of a Rock Dove is a bed of bloodstained feathers quivering in the breeze. Crows, however, constitute a big meal for a goshawk, so the less delectable body parts, such as mandibles and intestines, might be left behind.

The crows know where their nemesis lives and occasionally circle high above the goshawks' nest territory, spewing their scorn. I've also heard them make odd muffled calls in the vicinity of a crow kill, which I interpreted as lamentations for a family member. Why do they stay knowing that the goshawk owns the forest and that they are prime targets? Because their attachment to the land overrides their need for security.

To capture Rock Doves, which don't ordinarily inhabit forests, the goshawks raid bridges, I've concluded. Once I saw an adult male goshawk chase a Rock Dove up the middle of the

Housatonic—the goshawk catching up to the dove, the dove turning sharply at the last moment to avoid a thrust of the goshawk's talons, the dove pulling away, the goshawk catching up and thrusting again, the dove making another evasive maneuver. The death-defying moves of the dove convinced me this wasn't the first time it had dodged a goshawk. I was shocked to see the perfect killing machine miss, but then this goshawk may not have gone all out, perhaps because the dove saw him coming and lured him into the open. The goshawk prefers brief woodland ambushes to long pursuits over water.

I watched the chase until the birds were out of sight. I think the dove got away, because soon I heard the goshawk calling. If he had caught the dove, he would have been quietly tearing it to bits.

One of my oldest goshawk memories is the most distinct. I replay the encounter frequently. It happened in early March on the kind of day that convinces you spring is here for good. The sun was coming out after a rain, and it was so warm I felt like celebrating by walking in a new place with a favorite companion. At the time my sister Linda had a white German shepherd, Sasha. I borrowed Sasha and took her to Brett Woods in Fairfield.

The warmth of the sun had me looking forward to the season of easy living. Sasha sniffed along, filling her head with all the aromas of the awakening earth. At the bottom of a hill, a Black Duck, a Mallard, and three Wood Ducks—one male and two females—floated in a rainpool in the middle of the trail, a picture of sylvan repose. We couldn't detour around them—Sasha's leash would become tangled in the swampy woods bordering the trail—and I didn't want to turn back, so we pressed forward.

The Wood Ducks took off first, the females making their "loud distressed *whoo-eek*," as Peterson describes it. Just then a fourth bird materialized behind the wood ducks—a big silhouette slicing through the jungle of naked trees. It was the silhouette of a flapping goshawk.

The goshawk overtook the ducks in a few seconds. Swinging its talons forward, it struck one of the females in the chest and held fast. I heard the soft yet sickening impact. The two fell to earth diagonally, carried by the goshawk's momentum. The Wood Duck was still crying as they disappeared into a gully. Her companions were long gone.

I didn't follow for fear of forcing the goshawk to desert the kill. Satisfying my curiosity would have made a mockery of the duck's sacrifice. She hadn't given her life to become fodder for maggots. Now her body and spirit had to nourish her killer.

That I set the whole thing in motion haunts me to this day. I suppose the goshawk had been watching the ducks from a nearby tree, but for how long? Did the ducks know it was there, and that one of them was doomed?

I think the goshawk waited for Sasha and me to flush the ducks because picking one off the rainpool would have been too easy. The goshawk seems to relish the challenge of a moving target. Until the Wood Ducks flew, the chase impulse hadn't been stimulated. I suspect the panicked cries of the females only whetted the goshawk's appetite.

As I write this, a male Wood Duck and his mate cavort on the pond behind the house. He gives her a love bite, dives, surfaces, and beats his wings proudly. She answers with a brief cry, and with that I stick my head out the door. Whenever I hear the Wood Duck's cry, I remember the shattered calm of that March afternoon, and I'm compelled to search the air for the speeding figure of the brave and deadly goshawk.

CHAPTER 6

ICONS

THE BALD EAGLE AND THE WILD TURKEY ARE VERY DIFFERENT, YET THEY lead parallel lives and have had parallel histories. One is aerial, the other terrestrial. One lives on the river, the other on the leafy ground next to the river. Both birds were persecuted, both came back from near extinction. The two contended for the title of national bird of the United States. Although the turkey wasn't chosen, it became a quasi-national bird in its own right, however dubious the distinction. The likenesses of no other American birds are so instantly recognizable.

A few winters ago I proposed to a fellow birder that we compete to spot the Saugatuck Reservoir's first Bald Eagle of the season. The loser would buy the winner a case of beer. We'd proceed on the honor system, but there could be no doubt about the identification. A huge bird of prey soaring in the distance— merely a probable Bald Eagle—would not count.

When my friend declined my wager, I thought it was because he felt outclassed by my greater birding experience. Time, however, would humble me. Soon after I issued this challenge, he not only had found the season's first eagle but had also seen others: a total of four—two adults and two immatures, distinguishable by differences in coloration—compared with my total of zero.

To my further chagrin, I was unable to locate any eagles each time my friend called to describe the whereabouts of his latest sighting. The reservoir covers 868 acres, but even in this large area a bird with a seven-foot wingspan is no needle in a haystack. With a white head and tail sandwiching a dark brown body, the adult Bald Eagle is, in Roger Tory Peterson's words, "all field mark." Yet this unmistakable feathered giant continued to elude me.

To explain my inability to find eagles that winter, I came up with a theory. These fish-loving raptors visit Connecticut when advancing winter freezes their watery haunts to the north, the first eagles generally arriving by early December. They may remain into late March, but if enough ice forms, blocking access to fish and causing waterfowl to desert, and if no deer carcasses are available, the eagles seek prey or carrion farther south.

The Saugatuck Reservoir, large and deep, normally has considerable open water long after smaller and shallower Fairfield County reservoirs become solid ice. For years this characteristic had made the Saugatuck a magnet for a few wintering Bald Eagles, but the warmest winter in memory had left open other bodies of water. Not confined to the Saugatuck, the eagles could roam. While I searched for them at the reservoir, they might be miles away.

The theory was plausible enough; it was also a convenient rationalization for a frustrated birder. January had arrived, and still

I had not seen an eagle. Never had I gone so deep into winter without finding this spectacular bird. Some winters I have seen eagles on almost every visit to the reservoir, and once I had six in view simultaneously. This winter I hadn't found one in 15 tries.

I resolved to set aside a day for birding the reservoir and would not stop until I found *Haliaeetus leucocephalus*. The night before, I did a ritual cleansing of my binoculars and spotting scope. Then I disassembled the monopod I use to support the scope and cleaned the leg sections, washed and dried the nylon collars, and regreased the threads.

The next morning, armed with a special permit from the water company, I was at the dam a half hour after sunrise. The air was cold but still, broken only by the caws of reservoir crows and, in the white pines near my vantage point, the light tapping of a Downy Woodpecker. I checked all the favorite eagle perches: the spreading dead tree on the south end of the big island, the conifer groves jutting into the reservoir's east side, and the hemlock-covered sides of the hill above the dam. First with binoculars, then with scope, I did a 360-degree pan of the woods at the edge of the water. Not forgetting the sky, I scanned clouds and infinite blue.

I worked my way up the reservoir through the northeastern corner of Weston, stopping next at the wide "bay" south of Godfrey Road. The wind blew lightly from the north but carried no eagle into view. Farther along, I pulled into the boulder-strewn parking area just above the big island, a reliable observation post for eagles—until that winter. Binoculars around my neck, scope slung over a shoulder, I then walked the hiking trail between Valley Forge Road and the narrow channel at the reservoir's midsection.

I spotted other birds: Blue Jays and a Red-bellied Woodpecker, Buffleheads and a probable Pied-billed Grebe, a Red-tailed Hawk, and an unexpected Great Cormorant that slithered from the water like a feathered reptile and stood on a smooth slab of rock at reservoir's edge. I stopped to study three large birds soaring above a distant southern ridge, but their wings were uptilted—not spread-eagled almost flat against the sky—revealing them as Turkey Vultures.

I returned to my car and continued to Redding, where the northern third of the reservoir lies. From the next turnoff I chose, a downhill trail winds through woods before looping past the water. During the walk I persuaded myself to change my inner approach to this quest for eagles.

Nothing was wrong with my outer approach: I had put myself in the eagles' domain at a time of day when they begin to hunt. But like the hundreds of motorists who pass the reservoir on Route 53 every day without seeing eagles, my thinking was out of tune with the wild. I was focused like a laser in a world where discovery often comes by peripheral vision.

Looking at a tree, you hear a sound and want to see the bird that makes it. You stare hard and hear the sound again, stare harder but don't see the bird. From the sound, it must be right in front of you, but the branch is empty. If, however, you pull back and broaden the view to include the whole tree—even throw the scene out of focus—suddenly in the corner of your eye, you see the bird. It was there all the time, yet you wonder, how could you have missed it?

These thoughts helped loosen my perceptual bonds. Crossing a brook, I began to feel the reservoir, rather than just see it. With each step toward water's edge, my tunnel vision widened and the reservoir opened to me further. I became less conscious of being an outsider. A left turn off the trail brought me through a small stand of pines. Here I calmly accepted that today I might not see any eagles. I would stop trying so hard.

As I came out to the water, I felt the electric charge of other living things. Below this point the largely empty surface of the reservoir stretched for miles. But here, finally, there were hundreds of birds splashing around and filling the air with quacks and honks. Two hundred Mallard and twenty-five Black Ducks swam just north of where I stood, close to my side of the reservoir, many with heads underwater and tails tipped up. Thirty-five Canada Geese and a few Buffleheads floated in the middle, and a string of Common Mergansers paddled along the opposite shoreline.

Twelve more honking geese flew toward me from the other side of the reservoir, not in V-formation but one next to the other. This line of geese blocked my view of a bird that followed them, which for a second I took to be another goose lagging behind. When they banked to the left, the geese unmasked the bird in their wake: an adult Bald Eagle. Our meeting was a most satisfying culmination to my two-hour search that morning, plus all my previous attempts spanning several weeks. With an admiring nod, I welcomed this noble winter visitor to the woods and waters of southwestern Connecticut.

The eagle turned with the geese and followed them closely. It undoubtedly saw me standing on an exposed rock less than 200 yards away yet did not veer from its course. The fleeing geese honked anxiously, aware that eagles sometimes prey on their kind, but in this eagle's leisurely flapping I saw no intent to kill. It didn't impress me as huge, so I judged it a male, which can be 25 percent smaller than a female.

This lord of the air sailed north along the shoreline. Up went the large flock of Mallard and Black Ducks. They divided their number into smaller squadrons to create confusion and ready themselves for evasive action, but the eagle ignored them. The geese took a hard right turn across the water. The eagle let them go and continued straight toward the top of the reservoir.

Soon the ducks returned, chattering among themselves as they wheeled close by me before sliding into the water. Normally they would not come so near, but my threat was nothing compared to the danger they felt from above. I sensed their apprehension as the eagle, reaching the reservoir's northern brim, turned and slowly circled in our direction.

For a minute I lost sight of the eagle, then suddenly he materialized directly above the largest concentration of waterfowl. Ducks and geese frantically took to the air, zooming this way and that, yet the eagle showed no reaction. I wondered whether this was a hunting tactic designed to exhaust the prey before attempting a kill. Or perhaps this seeming lack of interest was a ruse that would change to a deadly surprise attack once a victim let down its guard. But would an eagle strike with a man this close? Perhaps I was the reason he would not show his talons.

All was commotion among the hundreds of waterbirds, yet high above the majestic eagle soared alone, tracing elegant circles in the clouds. The benevolent despot was, for the moment, overlooking his realm. He did not know and would not care that his image graces the great seal and the postal truck. He rises above all human matters, coming and going in silence, allowing us a glimpse before disappearing beyond the horizon.

After lording it over the other birds a while longer, the eagle moved south along the opposite shore, flying quite high. When he reached the expanse of water between the channel and the big island, he pulled back his great wings and rocketed down, finally displaying his predatory side. I thought he might have a trout in his sights. When he abruptly came out of the dive and resumed soaring, I knew the target had vanished.

By now this grand bird was a mere speck in my binoculars. I drove the four miles back to my starting point at the dam and viewed the eagle from another angle. At this distance his white head and tail were invisible against the clouds. Beyond him I saw other specks that represented large birds, maybe even other eagles. If they allowed me, and if I allowed myself, I would see them another day.

A few weeks later I took part in the Midwinter Eagle Survey, a count organized by federal and state wildlife departments. On the first day of the two-day count, I covered the Hemlocks Reservoir in Easton, where thick fog made viewing very difficult and recent rains had me trudging in deep mud. I could hear but not see the splash landings and water-pattering wings of gulls, geese, ducks, and mergansers. The few birds I saw would emerge from the mist as ghosts, then sink into a soft column of gray. It was hard to believe that on this weekend one year ago, my car got stuck in the snow.

After an hour of searching, I glimpsed an adult Bald Eagle through a momentary parting in the curtain of mist . Flying west toward the Saugatuck Reservoir, it disappeared behind a grove of shoreline pines. As I scanned for more eagles I heard the disso-nant sound of a human voice. An Easton police officer had come to check my credentials. He was satisfied by my special permit, though I sensed his displeasure at having to follow me through the mud.

For a midwinter day it was very mild, so I lingered to appreciate the strangely beautiful atmosphere. The sun was a disk of muted silver, and the zenith showed patches of blue. They should have named it Pines Reservoir rather than Hemlocks, because the trees looming above the earthbound clouds were mostly white pines. The fog crept along, encircling islands and filling shoreline indentations. It would lift or burn off, then reappear minutes later. Some birds seemed to feel protected by the palpable gray air: two Ring-necked Ducks floating near the shoreline, resting with bills tucked into their shoulders, let me pass without a hint of alarm.

The next day on the Saugatuck Reservoir visibility was no better, but by then I had learned how to bird in such conditions. If I kept to the hills, I could see above the water-hugging fog. At mid-reservoir I scanned the shoreline with my spotting scope and found an adult Bald Eagle in a bare tree on the water's east side. I felt successful enough, but when I heard its high-pitched cry, a sound usually reserved for other eagles, I thought it might have company.

My suspicion was confirmed on a hillside above the lower reservoir, where I found another adult. Immediately I drove back to the first eagle, which hadn't moved. Either of these eagles could have been the one I saw the day before at the Hemlocks. I was fortunate to find two, possibly three, eagles on the survey, because my later sightings that season were of solitary birds. By winter's end I would see four eagles at the reservoir—two adults and two immatures.

Late in the season the reservoir finally froze, and a big snow came, the white-laden trees camouflaging even adult birds, if any remained. One evening, as I walked along the reservoir on Valley Forge Road, no cars went by for an unusually long period. In the depths of pure winter silence, I listened for the eagle's call but heard only a cawing crow, the mournful honk of a Canada Goose, and the profound echo of shifting ice—an eerie, elastic sound. In some dark recess, amid giant trees and frigid air, feather-cloaked nobles of the reservoir slept.

A FIERCE DEMEANOR, A DISTINCTIVE WHITE HEAD AND TAIL, CRUSHING yellow talons, and an impressive wingspan endow the Bald Eagle with a majesty that few wild animals can equal. To the Second Continental Congress, this North American endemic seemed a fitting symbol for a republic founded on lofty democratic principles. On June 20, 1782, the Congress made the Bald Eagle an American icon by approving the use of its image on the great seal.

The decision incensed Benjamin Franklin, who had lobbied for the Wild Turkey. Looking through overly anthropomorphic spectacles, he became the eagle's greatest detractor. "He is a bird of bad moral character," Franklin said in a letter to his daughter, referring to the eagle's occasional practice of pirating fish from the Osprey. Because even the small kingbird seemed to attack the eagle without fear of reprisal, Franklin branded the national bird "a rank coward."

Time, of course, would prove Franklin wrong. In the minds of many Americans, the continent's second largest bird of prey (after the California Condor) has become synonymous with American ideals. Its image graces currency, stamps, art, architecture, and corporate logos. As the subject of more than 2,500 published papers and books, the Bald Eagle, moreover, is probably the most extensively studied North American bird.

Still, attitudes like Franklin's prevailed for the eagle's first 175 years as the national bird. Through the 1800s, the Bald Eagle's symbolic status did little to protect it from persecution. Settlers saw it as a competitor bent on depriving them of fish and game, and on depleting their livestock. They also killed eagles for sport. Sure, farmers and ranchers might have stopped to admire a soaring eagle. But then they reached for their guns. Meanwhile, Native Americans trapped and killed eagles to obtain ceremonial feathers. While shooting, trapping, and poisoning took their toll, the march of human progress was encroaching on the eagle's territory. Population growth and land clearing along navigable rivers and estuaries destroyed prime eagle habitat and caused declines in prey species.

Before European settlement, 250,000 to 500,000 Bald Eagles ranged across North America, and as late as the mid-1800s, wintering eagles reportedly fished the waters off New York's Manhattan Island by the hundreds, sometimes devouring their catch in Central Park. By 1940 the eagle's rarity compelled the U.S. Congress to pass the Bald Eagle Protection Act, which outlawed the killing and disturbing of eagles, as well as the possession of eagle parts, including feathers, eggs, and nests. After studies showed that eagle predation did not harm salmon populations, this law ended a bounty system in Alaska that claimed 128,000 eagles between 1917 and 1952. The actual number of slaughtered eagles probably exceeded 150,000, since many bounties were never collected.

For a long time the Bald Eagle Protection Act, designed also to protect the beleaguered Golden Eagle, was not strictly enforced. At one Wyoming ranch, for example, eagles were systematically shot for their perceived threat to livestock. According to a 1970 report, more than 770 Bald Eagles were shot at this ranch, and hunters got $25 for each carcass. Responding to a public outcry over such flagrant violations, the government began to crack down.

Just when it was finally benefiting from legal protections, the eagle took a heavy blow from DDT, a pesticide that enters the food chain and causes reproductive failure. Widely used after World War II to control mosquitoes and other insects, DDT was wreaking havoc among many bird species. Raptors were particularly vulnerable—over time, animals higher in the food chain accumulate more DDT. Rachel Carson exposed DDT poisoning in her 1962 book, *Silent Spring*. The United States banned the pesticide in 1972, but by then it had done grave damage. The eagle hit a low point in 1963, when a nesting survey in the lower 48 states found just 417 pairs.

The most sweeping protections took effect in 1978. Under the Endangered Species Act, the Bald Eagle was listed as endangered in 43 of the lower 48 states and as threatened in the remaining five. The estimated 50,000 Bald Eagles in Alaska are not at risk; therefore, they do not receive protection under the act.

Enforcement of the Endangered Species Act, and cooperation among wildlife agencies and conservation organizations on captive-breeding programs, led to a fourfold increase in nesting populations between the mid-1970s and mid-1990s. In 1995, the U.S. Fish and Wildlife Service downgraded the eagle's status in the lower 48 states to threatened. Now that there are more than 6,000 pairs of nesting eagles, with successful breeding reported in almost every state, the Fish and Wildlife Service has announced plans to "delist" the species entirely and is working out the details of a management plan. After delisting occurs, the Bald and Golden Eagle Protection Act and other legal safeguards at the federal level will remain in effect, and many states have laws that will continue to protect the eagle as an endangered, threatened, or "special concern" species. The current Bald Eagle population is estimated at 100,000; more than half the birds are found in Alaska and British Columbia. Although eagles will never be as abundant as they were before the arrival of Europeans, their comeback is one of the great conservation stories.

Their continued success requires vigilance, however. Threats include oil spills—the Exxon *Valdez* spill in 1989 killed some 250 eagles, and the local population did not recover until 1995. As humans encroach on eagle habitat, collisions with man-made structures and with vehicles are expected to rise. The National Wildlife Health Center is monitoring outbreaks of avian vacuolar myelinopathy, a fatal neurological disease that first showed up in Bald Eagles and coots wintering at an Arkansas lake in 1994. Twenty-nine eagles died that year. The disease has since been identified at lakes in four other southern states. Scientists don't know what causes it, but they suspect a man-made or natural toxin carried by waterfowl. They also suspect that eagles get the disease after preying on affected species.

They may be faring well on a national scale, but you still have to earn your eagles where I live, the fourth most densely populated state. Only a few pairs produced young in Connecticut last spring, and under state law the species remains endangered. More than a hundred eagles typically migrate from the north to spend at least part of the winter here, but the mild weather of recent winters has greatly reduced the numbers heading in this direction.

I credit warm winter temperatures, however, with giving me an unexpected glimpse into the eagle's private life. On a balmy afternoon in late February, nearing the crest of a hill overlooking the Housatonic River, I heard what I thought was a tree creaking in the wind. When I looked up, I realized the sound was a Bald Eagle's call.

Two adults, their heads and tails pure white, were circling rapidly just above the treetops, one chasing the other. For such huge birds, they wheeled about with amazing agility. The second eagle pulled even with the first. Then, moving with choreographic precision, the two birds turned their bellies to each other and, for a fraction of a second, they locked talons. The chase resumed, and the eagles disappeared into the river valley.

Talon-locking in eagles can be courtship or combat. I believe this was courtship, but I doubt the eagles were preparing to nest here. Triggered by the springlike day, they were probably rehearsing on their way to breeding grounds in Maine or Canada.

As their numbers grow, Bald Eagles can be expected to expand their breeding range, within limits imposed by habitat destruction, human disturbance, and environmental contamination. It is hard to imagine them nesting near my home on the fringe of busy Fairfield County. Still, every year, beginning about the time winter ends, I keep an eye out for eagles, hoping for the day they prove me wrong.

In late November my thoughts turn to that other bird with iconic status, but while most Americans think about eating turkey then, I think about seeing one—not the overweight, pale, domesticated bird that ends up on the Thanksgiving table, but its streamlined and bronzy wild ancestor. This ground-dwelling native of North American forests, so admired by Ben Franklin, is fairly common now, but only 30 years ago it was nonexistent across much of its historic range, a casualty of over-hunting and deforestation.

English naturalist John Josselyn was one of the first to note the turkey's decline. In 1672, after an extended visit to Maine, he wrote: "The English and the Indians having now destroyed the breed, so that 'tis very rare to meet with a wild Turkie in the woods." The estimated 10,000,000 turkeys that roamed North America before European settlement dwindled to a fragmented population of 30,000 by the early 1900s. They had been extirpated from 18 of 39 states they originally inhabited.

I glimpsed my first Wild Turkeys in the late 1970s at Aransas National Wildlife Refuge in Texas, but it took another decade for me to find them in my home woods. By then reintroduction programs in New England and elsewhere were proving success-ful. Members of remnant populations had been captured in rocket-propelled nets and moved to forested regions where no wild turkeys had been seen for a century or more. Sustained by good habitat—extensive, open woods with waterways and adjacent fields—and protected by hunting suspensions, many of the relo-cated birds thrived.

Wild Turkeys now occur in all of the lower 48 states, and their number has risen to more than 5.5 million. The male's gobbling once again begins ringing through the New England woods in late March, and each spring, as both sexes look for mates, they turn up in unlikely places. My mother, for example, called during a beachside walk in Westport to report "four huge all-brown birds much bigger than geese, with necks not as long—probably turkeys. They almost hit me in the head as they flew across the road."

To most observers, however, turkeys remain elusive. Their predators include Great Horned Owls, bobcats, cougars, coyotes, and foxes, so wariness is in their blood. Unleashed dogs take a heavy toll, and the return of turkeys has put their worst enemy—

human hunters—back on their trail. Getting close to a Wild Turkey on foot, therefore, isn't easy. My first Connecticut turkeys—five males that crossed my path in a nature preserve—behaved typically. When they saw me, they strutted away and took a hiking trail up a hill. I followed, trying repeatedly to get a good look, but they never allowed me more than a glimpse of their tails as they disappeared beyond the next bend.

Growing alarmed at my persistence, they peeled off the trail and ran down the other side of the hill, through some brush. Although I couldn't see them, their loud rustling kept me on track. I tried to stay within earshot, but my speed was no match for theirs, and I lost them along the border of a marsh.

Like most people, I've gotten some of my best looks at turkeys from behind the wheel of a car. They often forage in roadside fields or clearings, and they seem to view a car and its driver as a benign behemoth. As I drove to the Upper Paugusset State Forest late on a September day, two males in pitched battle stumbled into the road. They were in a shoving match, with necks entwined. Cars from both directions waited 30 seconds for them to move onto the road's shoulder, where, as I passed, I saw one lunge and bite the other.

Sometimes turkeys show contempt for cars, as did the female I met early one morning on a country road. She stood in the middle of the pavement with her brood as I drove up, and when I pulled alongside her, she didn't budge. Her reaction seemed to go beyond maternal protectiveness; it was as if she wanted to assert her dominance. I opened the window and respectfully tried shooing her to safety, which only made her angry. With spread wings, she adopted a threat posture and held her ground until another car approached from the opposite direction. Apparently feeling outnumbered, she finally led her young into the woods.

My cat had a similar confrontation in the driveway. Hollow knocks brought me to the door—the clucking of a female turkey. She and the cat were in a staring match, and it was the cat who blinked and withdrew. The cat tried to be nonchalant, but I think she was shaken, which made me suspect she had never seen the likes of a Wild Turkey. I knew one thing: she wasn't about to disturb the eight crow-size poults that lurked in the leaf litter behind their protective mother.

There was no adult male in sight, because the female assumes all the duties of nesting; the male's reproductive role begins with courtship and ends with mating. The female and young stay together through winter, often joining other broods to form large flocks. Adult males mix with these winter flocks, travel alone, or gather in their own groups. A winter flock might have 100 members, but in Connecticut flocks of 10 to 20 are typical.

The largest winter flock I've come across numbered 25 and included adult females, four or five adult males, and smaller birds that must have been born the previous summer. On a mild after-noon in early December, I had reached the midpoint of a trail through second-growth deciduous woods, and after crossing a stream heard an alarm call. I froze and saw a few turkeys head-ing away, up a hill. More foraged farther up, and others to the right were threading their way through shrubs and boulders.

Spread out across the hillside, the flock moved slowly to the left, noisily raking their feet through the leaves. When raking, the birds stood in place and pulled their feet back, the way we clean our shoes on a welcome mat. As they pecked the exposed ground for food—probably acorns and hardy insects—some ruffled their feathers, showing their salt-and-pepper primaries and secondaries.

My approach drove half the flock over the crest of the hill; the rest went over a stone wall to the left. Suddenly, I was alone on the hillside, and all was quiet. An eerie peacefulness pervaded the scene—had they really been here, these feathered dinosaurs? The proof was all around: dozens of bare circles of earth rimmed with leaves, a swath covering the full breadth of the hillside, bordered by a stone wall to the west, a road to the east. It was, I thought, an avian Stonehenge, and I had seen its creators at work.

CHAPTER 7

RARITIES

WITH A STIFF COLD WIND BLOWING OUT OF THE NORTHWEST, SHERWOOD Island was largely deserted. Even the model airplanes were grounded. The marsh grass waved beneath a sky the color of a Blue Jay's back. The morning sun had a dazzling brightness, as if polished by the wind. Although the chilly wind dominated, now and then I felt the sun's warmth and thought of summer. A birding companion and I had come to the park hoping to see something unusual on this blustery late-autumn day. I thought we might see a Golden Eagle heading south; my friend mentioned the White-winged Crossbill, a northern finch that very occasionally visits Connecticut. What we eventually found was neither crossbill nor eagle, but a unique bird with characteristics of both. Starting near the park entrance, we walked east along the reeds and shrubs separating the marsh from the dry fields. I said the park was deserted—of people but not of birds. Squadrons of Hooded Mergansers zoomed along the marsh's watercourses, Eastern Meadowlarks sprang out of the grass, Red-winged Blackbirds called as they flew by, and American Robins, hundreds of them, streamed almost continuously across the sky, oddly flying north. Two crows heckled a young Northern Harrier tilting over weedy fields in search of rodents. A lingering Great Egret hunted small marsh creatures along a muddy bank.

We had been birding half an hour, trailing sparrows along the shrubby marsh border, when my friend said he glimpsed "something good" dashing ahead of us. I peered over a wall of reeds and saw a gray-and-black bird with narrow white wing patches dive for cover in a lone cedar some 75 yards away. Although it resembled a mockingbird, I suspected something else and heard myself exclaiming, "It's a shrike!" The bird moved near the top of the cedar. Through our binoculars we saw that it was indeed a shrike, but most of it was obscured by foliage, and the light was against us.

We still had to determine whether it was a Loggerhead Shrike, a southern species, or its slightly larger and very similar relative of colder regions, the Northern Shrike. As far as we knew, neither species had ever been recorded at Sherwood Island. But to find out which it was, we needed a better look.

A game of hide-and-seek began. My eyes were riveted on the cedar as we approached the shrike, but when we reached the tree, it had vanished. We looked around in disbelief. How had it eluded us?

My greatest fear was that, flying low and out of view, it had turned north, crossing to the other side of the marsh. If the shrike had put the marsh between itself and us, even if we could spot it, we'd never be able to make a definitive identification at such a distance.

We backtracked to where we first flushed the shrike and retraced our steps. By the time we reached the cedar again, the wind had whisked away my hopes. Suddenly my friend shouted, "There it is!" Bounding through the air, the shrike landed in a cottonwood just behind the beach. It had remained there the entire time, quietly waiting for us to call off the search. Giving the wary shrike a wide berth, we followed it to a white birch, then back to the marsh edge, where at last we had some fine looks through our binoculars. It was an adult Northern Shrike, a robin-size bird with a heavy hooked bill, narrow black mask, silvery back, and finely barred underparts. Loggerheads have a smaller bill, fuller mask, darker back, and no barring. The Northern Shrike appears rarely in southern New England, arriving only when lack of prey forces it south of its normal boreal range. Although a songbird, it acts like a hawk, feeding in winter on small mammals and birds. Like the Loggerhead, it impales its prey on thorns, a habit that has earned them the nickname "butcher-birds."

I watched the shrike make a foray into the marsh. Hovering like a kestrel, it appeared to be hunting mice. Its usual flight pattern was a series of quick rises and dips. Before landing, it would plunge toward the ground and, at the last possible moment, angle up to its perch. My final glimpse was of it diving into a thicket, perhaps in pursuit of sparrows.

With half the park yet to bird, we moved to the west side. The wind grew more intense, but it did not affect me. I was thinking about Northern Shrikes and other winged rarities.

THE BRIDGE RISES SO HIGH IT TAKES ME NEARLY TO THE CLOUDS, AND I feel like I'm in a plane over the great inlet. At the apex I'm even a little hesitant to look over the side, because I might become dizzy and go veering off in my car. Peacefully I would plunge into the vast sheet of shimmering blue known as Narragansett Bay. Two hours ago, I decided on this mild and sunny January Sunday to drive to the Atlantic Ocean. Crossing the Newport Bridge, I'm bound for Rhode Island's Sachuest Point National Wildlife Refuge, perhaps the best place on the Northeast coast to observe wintering Harlequin Ducks.

There are an estimated 1,800 Harlequin Ducks in eastern North America. All breed in Canada, primarily along torrential mountain rivers in the north of Labrador and Quebec—the only bird species in the East that exploits this habitat niche during the nesting season, when it feeds mostly on aquatic insects. Eastern Harlequins winter off Atlantic Canada and the coast of the northeastern United States, nearly half of the population along Maine's Penobscot Bay and less than a tenth concentrated at Rhode Island's Sachuest Point.

Sachuest Point is in Middletown on Aquidneck Island's southeast tip, a short drive from downtown Newport. I pass a beach where surfers in wet suits paddle into winter waves, and as I draw near the refuge, buildings disappear and the ocean-washed lowland unfolds. My excitement builds as I turn right at a fork and follow a sandy road straight into the refuge parking lot. Although close to civilization, Sachuest Point feels isolated—a mound of low coastal vegetation fronting the Atlantic, between Sachuest Bay to the west and the Sakonnet River to the east. Comprising about 250 acres, with its southern end encircled by a nature trail, it is small for a national wildlife refuge and can be covered on foot in a couple of hours, yet I will learn that the saunterer seeking escape can lose himself in its concentrated wildness.

I ask a birder returning to his car where I can find the Harlequin Ducks. He points past an observation platform to the sea and simply says, "Nice!" I cut through shrubbery and emerge onto a promontory that plows the waves. Some 50 feet below and 150 yards offshore, just beyond waves and salt-sprayed rock, the dark and chubby Harlequins are the first birds I see.

I set up my scope with nervous hands, fearing they will move before I can get a closer look. It's a needless urgency. Glancing around the point I see several rafts of Harlequins. Although constantly in motion—riding the waves, diving for mollusks and crustaceans, flying back and forth along the shoreline—they are invisibly tethered to this rocky coast. These crashing waves and swirling waters are their temporary home, an unfrozen substitute for the rushing streams and turbulent rivers of Canada.

Among birders, Harlequin sightings are highly prized. Almost unheard of on my home waters of Long Island Sound, Harlequins are found at Sachuest in an exceptionally large concentration. At other Atlantic vantage points—such as Cape Ann, Massachusetts; and Long Island's Point Lookout and Montauk Point—you can see a few Harlequins if you're lucky, but here I've already counted 60 and a passing birder tells me there are more than 90.

Like the breaking waves that overwhelm the land, the power and stark beauty of the refuge overwhelm the human visitor. I'm sure a cold day on the point can be brutal, but despite what the calendar says, this midwinter day is downright balmy, with light breeze and brilliant sun. The air is pure, and the pounding surf produces a clean white foam. When the bubbles disperse, the water is tinged with turquoise, so clear I can see the Harlequins' paddling feet. Farther out the water turns ocean blue, and in the ear there is always the fresh sound of water meeting rocks. Nature smiles on Sachuest, and the Harlequins, cavorting in the surf, seem to know it. Do I hear one confirm this with a high-pitched whistle?

I want to explore Sachuest for other wild treasures, but I'm stuck on the Harlequins, with a grin on my face, incredulous that my count has risen to 90, the birds almost evenly divided between males and females. Harlequin Ducks are not the only rarity found here in numbers. Along the refuge's Ocean Ridge Trail comes a steady procession of scope-toting birders. It's as if I'm on another planet, where Harlequin Ducks and serious birders are the dominant life-forms.

All of the birders I speak to are Rhode Islanders, and many are as excited about the Harlequins as I. One is rightly proud that her tiny state has such a big attraction for out-of-town birders. Another, however, is far from awestruck. She asks, "Is there anything here besides Harlequin Ducks?"

A small group of Harlequins, only yards offshore, is being photographed by a woman perched on a wet boulder. Surprisingly tame, they don't seem to fear her and make no effort to move away. They may be curious about her, one of the many flightless vertical creatures who shun water and follow them all along the refuge shoreline.

Histrionicus histrionicus—the Latin name aptly describes the entertaining Harlequin. The male's black, gray, chestnut, and white plumage lacks the intensity and garishness of the Wood Duck, and even the Mallard has more vibrant hues. Still, the Harlequin appears wildly colorful. The reason is the male Harlequin's bizarre patterning. His white crescents, circles, and rings give an impression of color that he does not actually possess. A female nips a male; perhaps she sees through his imposture.

Most of the Harlequins stay just beyond the breakers, but now and then one rides inside the arc of a wave or dives under a wave that is about to break. Like many diving ducks, they take a short vertical leap before entering the water, which must give them momentum and allow them to enter cleanly. For a small duck they seem heavy in flight, and resting on rocks they look graceless. Once in the water, however, they are Olympian swimmers with abundant personality.

Finally I tear myself away from the Harlequins and walk east along the Ocean Ridge Trail. Eighty Purple Sandpipers—an unusually large assemblage of this species—rest on the massive offshore boulders known as Island Rocks. On Long Island Sound, Purple Sandpipers usually occur singly, where they occur at all.

Reversing direction, I come around the tip of the point to Sachuest Bay. As gulls sing an anthem to the sun, a man and a woman stand motionless and watch its flaming descent. In the darkening water I count at least a dozen Common Loons and glimpse the whiskered face of a harbor seal bobbing between waves.

Although I search carefully, I can't find other specialties of the refuge, such as the Short-eared Owl, Snowy Owl, Northern Harrier, and Barrow's Goldeneye. I do find Common Eiders—much rarer on Long Island Sound than they are here. There are many Red-breasted Mergansers and Common Goldeneyes, some White-winged Scoters, and a few Surf Scoters. Skulking in the coastal scrub are a Gray Catbird, Myrtle Warblers, White-throated Sparrows, and American Tree Sparrows. Herring and Great Black-backed Gulls are common, but I see no Ring-billed or Bonaparte's Gulls. In the logbook at the refuge building, visiting bird clubs have recently noted Northern Gannets and Razorbills, but if still around these birds escape me.

In a race with departing light, I follow the circular trail to an observation platform on Flint Point. To the northwest, silhouettes of Ruddy Turnstones glean the curving shoreline of the gently lapping Sakonnet River. It is after sunset when I return to my starting point. There I see 75 Harlequins, the largest single flock of the day. As darkness and cold settle over the waterscape, a couple asks whether I've seen any seals, and a final birder marches past.

The light fades, but the vast ocean heaves and crashes with the same intensity. Other birds have gone to night roosts—I stand on shadowy edge of land, alone with Harlequins and unrelenting sea. Soon the Harlequins rise together darkly and fly straight toward the ocean, perhaps to spend the night safely on an island in the distance. I'm pleased to think that today I may be the last person to see them.

The Harlequin Duck doesn't qualify as a bird of the decade. Nor does the Northern Shrike. By my definition, a bird of the decade must not only be rare; it must also have shock value. I have yet to see this decade's bird, but so far all my decade birds—one in the nineties, two in the eighties, and one in the seventies—have been large. Their grandeur, compounded by their rarity, left me speechless.

My bird of the nineties appeared on a hot morning in mid-June. I had pulled to the side of an overpass that gives a view of Sherwood Mill Pond, as I'd done hundreds of times before on my way into Sherwood Island State Park. Exiting the car, I saw something huge and white move on the pond's breeze-blown surface. It seemed to be sifting through the seaweed with the sword-like orange appendage at the front of its head.

I knew what it was before I raised my binoculars, but even as I focused I refused to believe it. Some kind of a hoax, I thought, as I envisioned chuckling conspirators pulling a mask over the head of a subdued swan. My pounding heart at last pumped enough blood into my brain to bring me back to reality. I was looking at an American White Pelican.

The last time I'd seen white pelicans was along the Gulf Coast, where many winter, but even there such dinosaurian birds seem out of place. They breed in colonies on lake islands, mainly in the prairie provinces of Canada and in the north-central to northwestern United States. In recent decades, single individuals have increasingly wandered into southern New England during spring, summer, and fall. White pelicans are built for soaring, which may partly explain their nomadic tendencies.

The tidal pond where this one had settled—next to the Metro North tracks and I-95—made my sighting that much more implausible. What could I do for proof? Lacking a camera, I needed eyewitnesses. I jumped into the car and barreled down to the park office. There I found two willing recruits: the park manager and a patrol officer. While they went to look at the pelican, I called two birders.

When I came back outside, the pelican had moved to a mud island. Four park employees joined me in watching it from an observation platform at the edge of a marsh. Soon another birder arrived. We were a small but happy crowd as we peered through scopes and binoculars and commented on the pelican's size and rarity.

An adult in breeding plumage, it had a keel, or centerboard (two parted, as I recall), on top of its bill and a shaggy crest. Its bill and pouch were deeper orange at the base, and the orange skin around its eyes had a bluish black border. It seemed relaxed. I saw it preen, swim, and stretch its black-tipped wings.

Other big birds lounged nearby—a Double-crested Cormorant, a Great Black-backed Gull, and two Mute Swans—but the pelican dwarfed them. Although a white pelican weighs a good six pounds less than a Mute Swan, the pelican's 108-inch wingspan beats the swan's by almost three feet. In North America, only the California Condor has a wingspan equal to or longer than that. Like the condor, the pelican seems very bulky when perched because it has so much wing.

As the morning temperature climbed, heat waves rising from the marsh obscured the views through our optics, so we moved to a parking lot that brought us roughly parallel to the pelican and to within 250 yards of it. A line of trees between the lot and the marsh gave us camouflage. It wasn't a bad setup, but it didn't last.

To our right, a birder came trudging into the marsh, headed straight for the pelican. We yelled and waved him back. He turned to us and pointed to the great white bird with a smile that seemed to say, "Can you believe this?" When he finally withdrew, it was too late. The wary pelican took off from the mud island. It circled and returned to the water, but a minute later it took off again. This time it circled much higher, then flew west and north, perhaps following the river up to the Saugatuck Reservoir. That was at 10:35, and it was the last we saw of it.

In my report to the Rare Records Committee of the Connecticut Ornithological Association, I noted that my sighting from the overpass at 9:20 had been the first. Later I learned this wasn't true, not by a long shot. Searching the Internet, I found a question on a birding message board from a man who had seen a white pelican the week before from the exit 18 ramp of I-95, which skirts the top of Sherwood Mill Pond. He wondered whether his sighting was unusual. I answered that it was very unusual indeed.

Although surrounded by houses, a highway, a railroad, and a busy state park, Sherwood Mill Pond has been a haven for other rarities. Standing tallest among them was a Sandhill Crane. As we fanatics sometimes put it, the crane was my bird. I was the first to see it (at least there's no Web evidence to the contrary), and it alternated between two of my favorite haunts. After spending the night in the pond, it went to work each day a few miles to the north in the fields of Wakeman's Farm.

In Connecticut, a Sandhill Crane is as rare as an American White Pelican. This lonesome drifter was off course by maybe a thousand miles—the nearest wintering populations are in Tennessee. By virtue of its rarity and size, the crane ranks as one of my birds of the eighties.

It appeared at 3 p.m. on New Year's Eve. I had borrowed my sister's dog Sasha for our customary walk around Isaac Wakeman's cornfield. The path into the farm leads over a pile of stones. We scrambled over them, and as we entered the field, the stuttering trumpet of a crane issued from amid the withered cornstalks. Then a bird standing as tall as a teenager leaped into the air. It took a turn around the field as it gained altitude, and off it flew. The crane beats its broad wings, which have a spread of up to seven feet, with a distinctive upward flick—the upstroke is quicker than the downstroke. Viewed from the side, the body of a flying crane is a series of sweeping curves formed by its long, outstretched neck and legs, and its hunched back.

The birder I called as soon as I got home already knew about the crane. He was the expert on rarities, the man everybody thought of when one appeared. He'd just gotten off the phone with a birder who lives next to Sherwood Mill Pond. The crane had landed there at about 3:15.

For almost two months, the crane stayed in Westport and stuck to its schedule—feeding at Wakeman's, sleeping at the mill pond. Those of us who waited for it at the pond always knew when it was coming. At about 4:30 p.m., all of the other birds on the pond would go up, including hundreds, sometimes thousands, of gulls. Then, on the northern horizon, the bird with the eagle-size wingspan that they had mistaken for a predator would come into view.

The crane usually settled on one of the pond's grassy islands, affording fine views to the many birders it drew from all over Connecticut, and from New York, Massachusetts, and Rhode Island. Now and then I met one of these rarity chasers skulking around Wakeman's Farm.

After I found the crane, I didn't visit it much at Wakeman's, where it was very skittish. The cornfield wasn't big enough for both of us. I still took my sister's dog there, but only after dark. Other people saw the crane until February 21, but my last sighting was on Valentine's Day, an appropriate date considering our bond: Of all the cornfields in Connecticut, it had chosen mine.

My other bird of the eighties, an immature bald eagle that appeared one winter day in Saugatuck, a congested coastal section of Westport, also stayed for weeks, and sometimes it visited the mill pond. No bird I've ever seen caused so much excitement in the nonbirding populace, I suppose because the bald eagle is the symbol of the United States, and in those days—early 1981— the eagle's dramatic recovery was just beginning.

I lived two blocks from where the eagle took up residence. Most days it could be found on the Saugatuck River between a steel bridge, which carries local traffic, and the I-95 bridge, which crosses the river on giant pedestals. A fishmonger on that section of the river threw scraps onto the ice for it. The eagle also fed on gulls and ducks. I photographed it with what appears to be a gull in its bill, and once I saw it chase a Mallard in circles. Quacking desperately, the Mallard dove into the water and the eagle passed over it.

At times, the eagle brought traffic on the steel bridge to a standstill as rubbernecking motorists strained for a look. Television news crews and radio stations did stories about the "American" Bald Eagle (there's no other kind) that showed up in the suburbs for no apparent reason. A photo in the local newspaper captured the eagle sitting on the railing of the mill pond footbridge, with a suspicious cat looking on. People in the neighborhood swelled with pride. When I told another shopper in Peter's Bridge Market that a Bald Eagle lurked just outside, she shook her head in amazement and declared, "Westport has everything!"

Since I lived so close to the eagle, I went to see it often and made a project of photographing it in incongruous settings. I snapped it flying past buildings and perching on a house near the mill pond. When I took the house shot, I was part of a small gathering of eagle-watchers on Old Mill Beach. The eagle sat on the peak of the roof and occasionally smoothed its chest feathers with its bill. "He's pruning," announced one man. Like many suburbanites, he must have had landscaping on the brain.

The eagle had moments of remarkable tameness. Twice it let me take pictures from the base of the tree in which it perched. During one of those sessions, I learned that closer is not always better in bird photography. I got my best shot when the eagle flew from the tree and landed about 200 yards away on the frozen Saugatuck River.

Three crows followed it onto the ice. The eagle raised its great wings in a threat—the decisive moment captured by my picture—and in another moment the crows were gone. Although the photo seems to depict the North Woods, it was taken in the shadow of I-95. That was more than 20 years ago, but the eagle might still be out there—Bald Eagles can live for over 25 years, and since about 1980 they have been benefiting from long-overdue protections.

The California Condor, my bird of the seventies, hasn't fared nearly as well. Shootings, lead poisoning from ammunition-ridden carcasses, and poisoning from bait used to control predators brought the condor to the brink of extinction by the mid-1980s. By 1987, all of the world's 27 condors had been rounded up.

Captive-breeding programs have increased the population to more than 200. Since 1992, condors have been reintroduced to southern California, the Grand Canyon region of Arizona, and Baja California, Mexico. (There are also plans to release condors in New Mexico.) No reintroduced population has become viable. Lead poisoning remains a leading cause of death in recently released birds. Reintroduced condors have also been lost to collisions with man-made structures, drowning, predation by Golden Eagles, shootings, and antifreeze poisoning. All three condor chicks born in the wild during 2002 died.

Twenty-five years ago last July, when an estimated 30 California Condors remained, I went to Los Angeles to visit my brother Ken, who was teaching a summer philosophy course at UCLA. I've introduced a few people to birding, but Ken took to it more enthusiastically than the rest. As the kid brother, I've always gotten the hand-me-downs. Birding is the one thing I've handed up. Ken is much more of a traveler than I, so his life list quickly surpassed mine. Today he lives in suburban Boston. Now and then we meet to chase down a rarity, a tradition that began in the mountains outside Los Angeles.

It happened that the chairman of UCLA's philosophy department, Bob Adams, was also a birder. He invited us to go with him to Los Padres National Forest in search of the condor. I sat in the back seat of Bob's Volvo. I remember the make because I've never been more impressed with a car's suspension. It took everything the rocky road up Mount Pinos could dish out. Bob drove at a clip that appalled me. My head was hitting the ceiling. No doubt the trip shortened his car's life span by several years, but it was worth it.

John Burroughs, the great nature writer of New York's Hudson Valley, said that "you must have the bird in your heart, before you can find it in the bush." The condor must have been in the hearts of my philosopher companions, because it wasn't in mine. Condors were so few then that chances were slim we'd see any. I didn't have big expectations. Nor did I have pen and paper. My brother's notes provide the details of time and place that follow.

At 11:45 a.m. on July 30, soon after we reached Iris Meadows on Mount Pinos, Ken pointed at two large birds in the distance. Bob was the first to get them in his binoculars. "It's ... It's ... the California Condor!" he proclaimed. The condors passed over us slowly. We lay down on our backs to take in their nine-foot wingspan and their distinctive white underwing pattern.

We continued up the mountain and saw two more condors from another meadow near the summit. At the summit's observation point we saw four—perched on snags and in the air. One perched condor was sunning with spread wings, a characteristic pose.

After all this time I can clearly recall the condor's hugeness. It soars steadily on flat or slightly raised wings and has seven long primary feathers, or "fingers," that curve up. Much larger than an eagle, it could from a distance be mistaken for a plane. I watched one fly out from the summit and "flex"—take a single, slow, downward wingbeat. Condors flex as they enter a glide, and the tips of their bowed wings nearly touch. The flexing condor seemed to gain great speed as it descended into a valley.

Aside from the condor, I saw nine species on that trip that I'd never seen before, including Clark's Nutcracker, Mountain Chickadee, Pygmy Nuthatch, Rock Wren, and Mountain Bluebird. Had I not seen the condor, I'm sure these western species—rarities only in the sense that they were new to me—would have made more of an impression. But all I retain is a vague recollection of them, and a check mark next to a name on my life list.

So it goes with many of the rarities I've seen close to home. They wandered into Connecticut and caught someone's eye. Word passed from birder to birder, and once the insiders got their looks, the rare bird alert spread the news to a wider audience. I pursued my share of such rarities, sometimes collecting a new check mark, the birder's equivalent of a hunting trophy.

My rarest Connecticut birds: Sharp-tailed Sandpiper and Ross's Gull. I photographed the sandpiper as it was mist-netted, measured, banded, and released at a coastal park in Norwalk. Why the fuss? It was the first definitive Connecticut record of this species, which breeds in Siberia.

When I look at my photos of the distressed sandpiper, however, I feel sorry for it, and a little guilty. It had committed no crime by flying halfway across the world and joining Pectoral Sandpipers in the park's rainpools. But it did get noticed by one of the state's best birders, who asked me, another photographer, and a bird bander to document its visit.

The Ross's Gull, an arctic species, was also a first for Connecticut when it showed up at the mouth of the Oyster River in Woodmont. I had my camera then, too, but the gull was out of range, so I focused on the throng of birders. A boy came out of the background and asked me what everybody was looking at.

"A very rare bird called a Ross's Gull," I said.

"Wow," he said. "All these people looking at a bird? I bet if I caught it someone would pay a lot of money for it."

A natural reaction from a boy, but was my behavior any different? I had arrived with a carload of birders and our purpose, in essence, was to bag a Ross's Gull. Rare and fantastic animals can bring out the worst of the possessive instinct. In the movies, it drove Carl Denham to capture King Kong. The instinct's tragic flaw: You may kill the object of your desire, as Denham did indirectly, or you may make it disappear, as we birders did the pelican on Sherwood Mill Pond.

Nowadays I seldom check the rare bird alert, and I don't automatically jump when I learn of a rarity by word of mouth. Yes, I'm waiting for the bird of this decade—my bird, not someone else's. I won't look hard for it, and when I find it I'll leave it alone. Until then I'm content to explore all that is rare and wonderful in the birds outside the door.

CHAPTER 8

FEEDER WARS

Be not forgetful to entertain strangers:
for thereby some have entertained angels unawares.
HEBREWS

THE BIRD FEEDER IS THE SUBURBAN EQUIVALENT OF THE AFRICAN WATER hole. It attracts many of the birds in the neighborhood, including some you might not otherwise see. More birds stop off in their migrations. Most come to eat seeds and suet, constantly jockeying for a position at the table. Sharp-shinned Hawks and Cooper's Hawks come to eat other birds.

To have a popular feeder, you must choose the right foods and provide them consistently. You must prevent gray squirrels and other interlopers from taking over. You must keep the feeder clean and the area safe. It's worth the effort. I don't need the animal channel. The struggle for survival plays out at my window. There I see more wildlife drama than I ever see in the deep woods, and I can study birds any time I choose.

This morning, for example, I pause to admire the uncommon beauty of a male Common Grackle. He stands on the tray feeder bathed in sunlight. No field guide can convey him adequately, because his metallic sheens change from moment to moment as he shifts position in relation to the sun. The greenish blue cast of his neck goes on and off. He bends and his inner-wing feathers turn violet. Golden flecks on his shoulders come and go. Now he is largely purple, but he swivels slightly and goes black all over. He changes his armor of bronze, green, blue, violet, and purple with a cock of the tail.

The White-throated Sparrow is no such quick-change artist. This bird becomes beautiful over time, as winter dissolves into spring. It, too, is common, outnumbering all other feeder birds except the Dark-eyed Junco, but in its dirty brown nonbreeding plumage it is easily overlooked. Not so the sparrow's spirited song, which makes the coldest and dreariest day bearable.

White-throated Sparrows feed under the pine throughout the day. The cardinal joins them at dawn and dusk. In the evening, as the sparrows settle amid the tangles near the pond, they repeat their flat call, which reminds me of an out-of-tune piano key.

There are two forms, or morphs, of the White-throated Sparrow—one with a tan-striped crown, the other with a white-striped crown. The sexes are similar, but in mid-April the male white-striped form acquires the most impressive plumage. The white on his throat and crown, a sickly beige in winter, turns pure white. The blurry streaks on his gray breast disappear. The yellow spots in front of his eyes brighten. He is no longer the feeder wallflower. He is looking good and he knows it. Of all the common feeder birds, only the American Goldfinch undergoes a comparable spring transformation.

I watch the grackle and the White-throated Sparrow, among others, through a glass door to the left of my desk. The tray feeder is mounted on a pole next to the trunk of an Austrian pine 15 feet from the door. More feeders hang from the pine's lower branches. Another stands outside the window over my desk. My binoculars sit at the ready a few inches above my keyboard.

My path to power feeding began with a small wooden feeder, a homemade affair that I filled with black-oil sunflower seeds. I put it up outside the desk window in late fall and took it down in early spring. It had a limited number of avian visitors because gray squirrels monopolized it.

When the squirrels took a break the birds would appear. My notes recall a typical succession of visitors. A male House Finch arrives. The picky type, he rejects several seeds after feeling and sounding them. Finding one that will do, he deftly cracks the shell and strips away piece after piece solely by manipulating his bill.

Next comes a male junco. He throws seeds into the window with his bill and rakes the floor of the feeder with both feet. He rakes not to make a mess. His behavior mirrors how he scratches for food on the ground.

Later a Song Sparrow lands on the feeder roof, and I notice it is reluctant to fly down to the perch. Song Sparrows are not the nimblest of flyers. It might be easier to reach the perch from below, so the sparrow decides to drop into a bush. But when it flies up it overshoots the perch and finds itself back on the roof. Not to be so easily defeated, the sparrow tries a different tack. Rather than flying straight down to the perch, it flies horizontally, going a few feet away from the feeder. Now the sparrow has room to maneuver. It comes back diagonally and finally lands on the perch.

Another day brings a small flock of House Finches. They line up on the perch and dine without rancor. A starling flies in and they scatter. The starling sweeps through the seeds, looking, I think, for one without a shell. Four more starlings join it. They squabble and leave.

Such were the wooden feeder's everyday visitors. In time I stopped observing them closely. Of one consistent visitor, however, I never tired. The wooden feeder excelled most of all as an amphitheater for performances of the White-breasted Nuthatch. While House Finches fed from the perch, the nuthatch, a male, would patiently wait his turn, hanging upside down from the roof. When the finches left he'd drop onto the perch, pick up a plump seed, and position it at the very tip of his bill. He'd turn around and lean forward. Just as he was on the verge of taking off, he'd hesitate.

His expression was deadpan, but I knew what he was thinking: I can do better. So he'd drop the seed, turn back toward the feeder, sweep his bill through the seed bin, and pick a new candidate. Nice one, I'd think. He'd turn away from the feeder and seem about to leap into the air. Then he'd get to thinking again. No, this isn't what I was looking for, after all. His mandibles would separate ever so slightly. Down the seed would go.

This happened repeatedly. From the other side of the window, I'd play the nuthatch guessing game. Could this seed be the one? Yes, yes, yes ... no! He'd never look down after dropping the seed. He didn't care where the rejects went.

Eventually he would find a seed that worked for him. Only the mind of a nuthatch could understand why. He'd lean forward. I'd hold my breath. And he was off! Usually, he flew only as far as the trunk of the Austrian pine.

To hatch the nut (hence the name), he wedges the seed into a crevice and hammers it with his bill. Chickadees and titmice typically hammer open a sunflower seed while holding it with their feet.

The nuthatch's habit of wedging it into a crevice seems to free him to work more effectively. He can come at it with more powerful blows, hammering it in the fashion of a woodpecker. He can twist it while both of his claws firmly grip the bark—the toes of one foot pointing up the trunk, the toes of the other foot pointing down.

The nuthatch chooses his crevices carefully. He may try wedging the seed here and there to find the perfect fit. Sometimes while he hammers, the sunflower kernel pops out of its shell and tumbles down the trunk. The acrobatic nuthatch is prepared. He will not have the immaculate kernel sullied by contact with the soil. He runs straight down the trunk and makes a catch worthy of a major league shortstop.

Out of habit, he may wedge into a crevice a seed that doesn't need to be opened. I saw him do so with a corn kernel. He was winding up to strike it when he realized his mistake. Without the least bit of embarrassment, he snatched the kernel from the crevice and swallowed it whole.

For weeks I thought this male was alone, but now and then he'd return to the feeder in less time than it should have taken him to open and consume a seed. I started looking more carefully. Occasionally, a different nuthatch showed up, one with a narrower black cap—a female. I had overlooked her because Peterson's field guide had taught me that females have gray caps. A check of other field guides revealed that Peterson wasn't entirely correct. Some females have black caps.

The male and the female were mates. The female came less frequently because male nuthatches dominate a winter feeding territory. Although often separated by more than a hundred yards—the male at the feeder, the female in trees near the stream— they traded contact calls, usually a double honk.

Warm days in late winter and early spring would bring out the male's romantic side. He would hitch down the trunk of the pine to the ground and pick up a sunflower seed. On his way back up the trunk, the female would hitch down to meet him, and he'd give her the seed. It appears a matter-of-fact exchange—the male cardinal, in comparison, feeds his mate with obvious affection—but for the undemonstrative nuthatch this is a tender moment. The male sang with equal tenderness. He would land on the wooden feeder's roof and pump up and down while producing a short series of sonorous rapid-fire whistles, a musical variation on the nuthatch's familiar series of nasal *yanks*.

Such performances ended when gray squirrels destroyed the wooden feeder. I replaced it with one designed to deter them— the counterweighted metal type. If a squirrel steps on the feeder's perch, a steel curtain connected to the perch comes down in front of the seed hopper. The same happens if flocking birds such as starlings or House Sparrows gather on the perch. These "undesirables" discourage the small, native songbirds that most people want to feed: chickadees, titmice, nuthatches, and goldfinches.

Although intelligently designed, the curtain feeder has weak points. If I don't keep the slippery metal roof free of snow, the squirrels dig in with their rear claws, hang their heads in front of the hopper, and without touching the counter-weighted perch, help themselves to the seeds. Otherwise, the feeder deters them effectively.

Raccoons are another story. Having a longer body than squirrels, they easily foil the curtain feeder by gripping the feeder pole with their hind legs. With the pole supporting their weight, they can bypass the perch and reach their dexterous hands into the hopper.

If I still fed birds only in winter, raccoons wouldn't be a problem, since they den up in cold weather. But now I feed year-round to attract Rose-breasted Grosbeaks, Indigo Buntings, towhees, and other breeders. When the temperature rises enough to bring out the raccoons, I padlock the steel curtain closed each evening.

In the course of a day, I suppose I glance at my feeders hundreds of times, a habit that may have saved the life of one male House Sparrow. I saw him flapping madly at the curtain feeder without going anywhere. When I went outside I found that he'd gotten his head stuck between the seesawing perch and the fixed lip of the hopper. I closed my hand around his body, pressed down on the perch to widen the opening, and out he came.

I held him a moment and felt the beating of his heart. The light in his eye told me he was uninjured, yet he was plainly terrified—if he wasn't, he would have tried to bite. His helpless look seemed to ask if I was going to eat him. I turned from the feeder and gently tossed him up. He flew straight for the trees. I felt power when I held him in my hand, even greater power when I let him go. Having the power to kill but choosing not to—that's what separates humans from other predators.

How did this freak accident occur? I imagine that the sparrow came to the feeder as part of a flock. The combined weight of the birds rapidly lowered the perch just as he was reaching for seeds. His head pitched forward and dipped below the perch. Facing a closed curtain, the other birds took off. Without the weight of the flock to hold it down, the perch snapped up and caught the sparrow under the neck. He was stuck—unable to pull his head through the narrow space between the raised perch and the lip of the hopper.

This hasn't happened again. Still, I've never warmed up to the curtain feeder. Neither have the birds. The unsteady perch seems to spook them, and they avoid landing on the slick metal roof. My pine feeders are more popular. They include two hanging tube feeders—one for black-oil sunflower, the other for thistle—a hanging suet feeder, and the pole-mounted tray feeder

All have cages designed to keep squirrels and large birds away from the food, though during raccoon season I must take them in at night or face a feeder wreck in the morning. The squirrels can't get to the suet, but they've learned that by swinging on the sunflower and tray feeders they can spill some of the seeds. That's a lot of work, so for the most part they're content to share in the seeds I spread under the pine for the ground-feeding birds. As an admirer of the beauty, agility, and persistence of gray squirrels, I like having them around, and this setup keeps them under control. They come and go, leaving the birds ample time to eat in peace.

I strongly advise anyone who feeds birds against using seeds laced with hot pepper to deter squirrels. The pepper comes premixed into some seed blends; it is also sold in pure, powdered form. I tried the powder in my old wooden feeder, and though I mixed the highest recommended ratio of pepper to seeds, I saw no decrease in squirrel activity. I did see a squirrel with a badly swollen eye, however, soon after I started using this product. Fearing for the ophthalmic and digestive health of my feeder visitors, I disposed of the product as I would any hazardous chemical.

Aside from thistle seed (which attracts mainly goldfinches) and suet (which attracts mainly woodpeckers and nuthatches), I offer the birds black-oil sunflower seed and white millet. I avoid packaged mixes, especially the supermarket variety, because most contain milo and other fillers that birds largely ignore.

The sunflower goes in the curtain feeder and in the hanging tube feeder. A mixture of sunflower and white millet goes in the tray feeder and on the ground near the pine. Sometimes I add safflower seed and peanut kernels to the tray feeder and to the ground mix. At the edge of the pond in the backyard, I spread cracked corn for the Mallard and Canada Geese. I've had little success with birdbaths. They can't compete with the pond.

In summer I refrigerate the suet overnight to prevent it from turning rancid. During very hot periods, I stop offering suet because Downy Woodpeckers tend to become dependent on it. They also may develop bare spots on their faces from overexposure to the grease.

Feeder traffic starts to wind down in midsummer, but I keep the restaurant open because I don't want to disappoint customers like the White-breasted Nuthatch. When I was feeding birds only in winter, a nuthatch came around on a July afternoon. First he inspected the pine, then he flew to my open window. The suet and wooden feeders had been down for months. He seemed to wonder what had happened to them. Don't tell me that birds don't remember.

Pet and feral cats prowl my neighborhood, and though several pass my door every day, they rarely stalk the birds because the feeder grounds are fairly open. This gives the birds a clear view of approaching cats; without cover, the sneaky cats see little point in loitering, and if they do I chase them away. Occasionally, I allow my own cat a supervised outing. If she starts to wander, or if I see a coyote, I bring her in. She's not particularly interested in birds at the feeder and has never killed one. No cat, however, can be trusted around a feeder. I learned this from sad experience.

A warm December morning brought a female Golden-crowned Kinglet to the pine. She hopped about the twigs and hovered at the needle tips. She slid one needle between her mandibles. To my eyes, the needles looked bare, but the kinglet gleaned food from them continuously. Whatever food it was, there was a lot of it.

Watching kinglets in the woods, I had often wondered what insects they find as they hover high in the hemlocks. This one, hovering at eye level, would at least tell me what a kinglet finds in an Austrian pine in early December. I clipped some of the pine needles and put them under a magnifier. They were covered with aphids—spruce or pine aphids, according to my field guide to insects.

The kinglet moved to a short ornamental evergreen in front of the house and let me approach very closely. I was tempted to photograph her, but the morning sun filled me with lassitude. I stretched out on the lawn next to the feeders. The House Finches and goldfinches wouldn't feed with me lying there, though the chickadees and titmice kept coming.

Seeing a neighbor's cat in the distance, I thought of the feral cats in the area and congratulated myself for creating a feeder environment they couldn't exploit. Soon I went inside to look for more information on aphids. A while later, as I passed the door, I noticed the neighbor's cat chewing something under the pine.

Probably a rodent, I thought as I stepped out to investigate. It was, however, a bird. The cat had devoured so much of it that I doubted I'd be able to identify it. Gray feathers suggested Tufted Titmouse, but then I found yellow ones. A feathery clump constituted what little remained of the body. I turned it over. It was the Golden-crowned Kinglet's head.

I was overcome with a dreadful feeling, one I knew all too well. A bird that barely an hour ago had graced my surroundings now sat in the stomach of a cat. A vibrant and seemingly happy creature had, on this beautiful day, suffered a horrible fate that could have been prevented.

I was partly responsible. I should have remembered that small woodland birds that pass through residential areas only during migration are especially vulnerable to cats. The Winter Wren is one such bird, and as a ground dweller it is at an even greater risk. The Golden-crowned Kinglet is another.

Kinglets breed and winter in coniferous woods, and you don't find many domestic cats in that kind of habitat. Cats are dangerous to virtually all birds, but those that live year-round in the suburbs—the Northern Mockingbird, for example—at least learn to recognize cats as predators. The Golden-crowned Kinglet is comparatively clueless.

There's a good chance the poor kinglet had never seen a cat. She might have been born the previous spring, and her first migration from the northern forest took her through my yard. She paid no mind to me, an unfamiliar creature that happens to pose little danger, and no mind to the furry creature with the flea collar, the one crouching next to the dwarf evergreen in which she was foraging. Presented with this unexpected opportunity, the cat took it, of course. The irony is that one of the cat's hind legs is badly deformed, which only underscores the need to prevent any cat from roaming, since kinglets and many other birds are clearly defenseless against even three-legged cats.

I was kicking myself. Why hadn't I stayed outside and watched that cat? Then I got angry—at the cat for killing this special visitor, and even at the wide-eyed kinglet for lacking a more sophisticated survival instinct. Most of all, I was angry at people who let their cats roam.

When a roaming cat kills a wild animal—whether it's a bird, rodent, shrew, rabbit, bat, snake, or amphibian—people often shrug and say, "That's nature." Well, there's nothing natural about it. In the wild, the domestic cat is an alien species, and none is more destructive to wildlife.

I make this charge from experience. For six years I had an outdoor cat, the same one that today I restrict to supervised outings. She has not made a kill in more than three years. Before then she terrorized the neighborhood. Here is my record of one cat's swath of destruction.

Mimi's Death Toll
21 masked shrews
19 meadow voles
15 eastern chipmunks
5 woodland voles
5 garter snakes
4 green frogs
4 short-tailed shrews
2 deer mice
1 pickerel frog
1 Tufted Titmouse
1 Winter Wren
1 Song Sparrow
1 Dark-eyed Junco

That's 80 kills, all native species. I'm sure I rescued at least 80 more from Mimi's clutches, and I did not let her out at night, so her death toll may be far less than that of the typical outdoor cat, of which there are an estimated 40 million in the United States. There are another 40 million to 60 million feral cats. Each year these 80 million to 100 million cats are believed to kill hundreds of millions of birds and a billion or more mammals.

Windows and glass buildings may endanger birds to an even greater degree. Birds seem to think they can fly through the trees and the patches of sky reflected in glass, which is why the outside surfaces of all windows near feeders (and any window hazardous to birds) must be covered with a screen, with a curtain, or with closely spaced opaque decals that tell birds the window is a solid object. In the book *Pete Dunne on Bird Watching*, Daniel Klem, Jr., a biologist who studies window kills, writes, "Sheet glass is very arguably the most underappreciated lethal threat to birds." He estimates that collisions with sheet glass kill up to a billion birds in the United States every year.

This staggering death toll implicates many of the 50 million Americans who feed birds. Window kills at houses rise in winter, the most popular bird-feeding season. If you fail to make your windows "feeder safe," you may be luring birds to their deaths. I use black decals resembling falcons, affixing them in a diving position to the exterior side of my door and window glass. I'm skeptical that the birds recognize the silhouettes, but the decals work. Fatal collisions here have become almost nonexistent.

MY FEEDER LIST STANDS AT 52 SPECIES. DURING MUCH OF THE YEAR, 15 to 20 core species visit almost every day—various woodpeckers, sparrows, finches, and blackbirds; chickadees, titmice, and White-breasted Nuthatches; Mourning Doves and jays. Yellow-bellied

Sapsuckers, White-crowned Sparrows, and Purple Finches are rare but regular migrants. Pine Siskins occur rarely in fall and winter during years in which winter finches invade.

One or two Fox Sparrows pass through in November as they go south, and in March as they return to their breeding grounds in northern Canada. This year, however, two stayed through the winter, and in mid-March four more joined them. Feeding shoulder to shoulder brought out their competitive instincts, and occasionally one erupted into song, a first for my ears.

Roger Tory Peterson found the Fox Sparrow's song "brilliant and musical"; David Allen Sibley describes it as "the richest and most melodious of all sparrows." What I heard was a short series of loud whistles sliding up and down, similar to a House Finch's song. It was neither musical nor melodious, but, according to Edward Howe Forbush, author of the classic *Birds of Massachusetts and Other New England States,* I wasn't getting a proper rendition. Fox Sparrows' "musical efforts in migration," he wrote, " ... are not to be compared with the full song as given on their breeding grounds."

Rusty Blackbirds have also appeared in fall and spring, but they are much rarer than the Fox Sparrow. Last December two males found a meal under the pine during a snowstorm, affording fine views of their golden nonbreeding plumage. This April, during another snowstorm, two males were again under the pine. Now they were mostly deep purple, with flecks of gold on their upper backs and breasts. Between feeding forays they sang from the trees along the stream, sounding like a cross between a Red-winged Blackbird and a grackle.

My shyest feeder birds are Wood Duck and American Crow, both cracked corn devotees. My largest feeder bird, the Wild Turkey, also ate cracked corn during its sole appearance. Other onetime birds include Ring-billed Gull, Northern Rough-winged Swallow (on the ground, pecking millet), Red-breasted Nuthatch, and a pair of Northern Pintail. The pintail spent part of a cold March day right outside the door. They came from the pond with a group of Mallard to vacuum up seeds I had thrown under the pine. The male nipped at the Mallard and at his mate. Pintail are an uncommon migrant in southwestern Connecticut—a notable species even on the coast. I had never seen a pair at such close range.

My best out-of-season bird was a Ruby-crowned Kinglet that stayed from mid-December to early February and fed on suet. In Connecticut the fall migration of the Ruby-crowned peaks in mid-October. It moves farther south by mid-November but lingers on the coast in small numbers until late December. It is rare in January and, at inland locations such as mine, almost unheard of in February. While the kinglet remained, I stocked the suet feeder religiously. Although the hardier Golden-crowned Kinglet can spend the entire winter in Connecticut and never partake of suet, I doubt that the Ruby-crowned would have survived without it.

Two weeks into its visit, I learned the kinglet was a male when he unveiled his ruby crown. After that he showed it often. The warm days of early January prompted him to *jibbet* approvingly, but in the latter half of the month he had to endure 12 days of morning temperatures that hovered around 0°F. He came to the suet in a 50-mile-per-hour wind. He came in a snowstorm that put a powdery halo on his crown. Perhaps I had been entertaining an angel unawares.

When I saw him at daybreak on February 1, I cheered his incredible endurance. A few days later, as I replaced the old suet cake with an unfrozen one, the ragged kinglet waited in the pine, two feet above my head. It was a relatively warm 20°F, and a White-breasted Nuthatch's song floated in on the breeze. The day before, I had seen 75 robins in the Upper Paugusset State Forest. I took these as signs that the kinglet would make it through the entire season.

On February 8, I watched through binoculars as he peeled little white slivers from the suet cake. In my field notebook, I wrote that he seemed fine. The next day, however, I looked for him in vain. The previous night had been very cold, but he was used to that, and in the afternoon the temperature rose into the forties. Either he didn't need the feeder anymore, or he'd had enough of the New England winter and went south. Of course, he could have just given up. Feeder stories often don't have endings.

Birds like the Ruby-crowned Kinglet, which come to the feeder singly, and sometimes in pairs, are among my favorites. The Red-bellied and Downy Woodpeckers, Northern Flicker, White-breasted Nuthatch, Carolina Wren, Field Sparrow, Eastern Towhee, and Rose-breasted Grosbeak—all have a bit of the loner in them, and being something of a loner myself, I identify with them more than with the sociable Mourning Doves, chickadees, titmice, American Tree Sparrows, Chipping Sparrows, White-throated Sparrows, and juncos.

I do have a soft spot for the gregarious birds of exceptional beauty: cardinal, Blue Jay, and goldfinch. No wonder British birders coming to North America for the first time place the cardinal and jay high on their list of desired species. They may not seek out the American Goldfinch with the same fervor, since the Eurasian Goldfinch is more colorful, but I prefer our breeding male. A yellow-and-black flower, he is showy but not gaudy.

The feeder's most understated beauty—in voice as well as appearance—may well be the Field Sparrow. White eye rings give it a big-eyed, vulnerable look. Its pink bill adds to this impression, seeming too delicate for cracking seeds. Delicacy also characterizes the sparrow's wistful song, which vies with the Prairie Warbler's and the Song Sparrow's for the title of perfect accompaniment to a dreamy summer day.

Although it has no song to speak of, the Ruby-throated Hummingbird vies with no one. A beautiful loner whose every action mesmerizes, it weighs slightly more than 0.1 of an ounce and is only 3.75 inches long (including a 0.65-inch bill), which makes it the smallest of eastern birds. The hummingbird's unique wing structure allows it to hover and to fly backward, sideways, and upside down.

A male arrives on May 1—the first hummingbird of the season. He is an iridescent green micro-torpedo, surrounded by a blur of wings. His wings beat about 80 times a second, and the muscles that power his flight account for nearly a third of his body weight. To meet the massive energy demands of sustained flight, his heart rate may rise to more than 1,200 beats a minute. He cruises at 30 miles per hour and reaches 60 miles per hour in a dive.

He slams on the brakes in front of my hummingbird feeder, which hangs in the pine. The feeder consists of a clear saucer with a red cover that has four openings, or ports. It holds 12 ounces of "nectar," a solution of one part white table sugar to four parts water (red dye is unnecessary), boiled and cooled. Never use honey or artificial sweeteners, which are poison to hummingbirds. I clean and refill the feeder every two to three days, sooner if the solution becomes the least bit cloudy.

A Ruby-throated needs about ten calories a day to survive. In the wild, flower nectar and insects provide this sustenance. Ten calories doesn't sound like much, but remember that the hummingbird weighs roughly 0.1 of an ounce. To get the equivalent number of calories in relation to my weight, I'd have to eat more than 700 macaroni and cheese dinners.

The hummingbird's body seems to swivel on the axis of his wings, causing his tail to swing this way and that as he shuttles around the feeder. When he screeches to a halt in midair, he looks quite the cartoon character. At first he moves from one feeder port to another, just as he would move between flower blossoms, but eventually he learns that he can stay at one port and drink his fill.

Sometimes he hovers when he drinks; at other times he perches. His throat patch, or gorget, appears black unless the light hits it at a certain angle—then it glints a deep metallic red. When the hummingbird has sipped enough sugar water, he doesn't take off with a leap, as other birds do. He revs up his wings, releases his grip on the perch, rises slowly, and levitates for a moment before shooting toward the woods or the wetland, where I lose him against a backdrop of green.

Knowing he'll return in minutes, I lie on my back under the pine. I hear the hum of his wings before he comes into view. The hum is loudest when he flies in; as he hovers it becomes almost imperceptible. Noticing me, he backs off and the hum momentarily rises. He eyes me, hovering an arm's length from the feeder, and I hear a querulous chip. In seconds he concludes that a leviathan such as me could not possibly catch him. He comes in for several quick sips. As he leaves he throws me a disdainful look.

A few days later I watch him feed in a hard rain. After taking his usual five or six draughts, he points his bill to the sky and opens it briefly, perhaps to take a drink or to wash away syrupy residue, and he shakes off the rain. Once he came to the feeder at dusk and inserted his bill in the ports 18 times, the most sips he's taken—stoking up, I suppose, for a cool night.

Well into the season, a female turns up. She probably has a nest nearby and may have mated with the male. She perches on the feeder and takes one long drink. I see her long needlelike tongue sewing back and forth into the sugar water. She returns twice. The male comes frequently that day, but I never see the two together. It's almost as if he were avoiding her, which seems odd since Ruby-throateds are known as pugnacious defenders of their feeding territories.

The male mates with as many females as possible, he does not form lasting pair bonds, and he normally takes no part in nesting. He does have a flight display, however, that rivals the woodcock's. On a glorious first day of summer, he performs it in front of the door, flying in a U-shape arc between the pine trunk and the window above my desk. Starting about 6.5 feet above the ground, and maintaining a fairly upright posture, he dives almost to earth before coming up near the house.

In frantic flight he went back and forth four times. The ends of the arc were about 25 feet apart. Although I did not see another hummingbird, the male performs this display either to impress a female or to intimidate another male. It may even be directed at people.

The hummingbird does not confine his aggression to birds and mammals. I have watched him spend an entire morning in a battle with a honeybee. Just as the hummer would get in position to feed, he would notice the bee on the feeder rim and give chase. The two would zigzag around. Thinking he had driven the bee away, the hummer would return to the feeder. Moments later so would the bee. A new chase would ensue, and the cycle kept repeating. The hummer wasn't trying to eat the bee. As if the bee knew this, it kept taunting. The hummer seemed to enjoy the diversion.

Hummer traffic increases at the feeder in August, when early migrants pass through and adult females visit with their young. I see more chases and hear more angry twittering, but now and then an adult male and female will surprise me by feeding together. A drizzly day in mid-August brings an adult female and a juvenile male. Except for a single fleck of ruby red on his mottled throat, the juvenile resembles his mother. He feeds next to her for a while, then moves to a pine branch and preens his back feathers with his bill. He cleans the bill by wiping it along the branch, against which it seems to bend. After scratching his head and fluffing his plumage, he settles down, keeping balance with an occasional buzz of the wings.

Only when it rests does a hummingbird approach the level of other birds. Otherwise, it is truly a meta-bird. I can't improve on John James Audubon's description: "This lovely little creature moving on humming winglets through the air, suspended as if by magic in it, flitting from one flower to another, with motions as graceful as they are light and airy...this glittering fragment of the rainbow."

I'M NOT COUNTING AMONG MY FEEDER 52 LIST THE FEMALE ZEBRA FINCH, a species native to Australia. On a summer afternoon, an unfamiliar sound reminiscent of a nuthatch's call brought me outside. There she was, eating millet—a little thing with an orange bill and feet, and black-and-white tail barring. The white patch below her eye, bordered with vertical black lines, imparts a teardrop effect. She fed alongside House Finches. Although she was different, they did not harass her.

While I stood on the walkway, she perched in the pine and on a stone wall, went to trees along the stream, and came back. The House Finches flew away, but she stayed. Clearly she was tame. I left the door open and tried to lure her inside with flattering words, but she was wise to my tricks. She wasn't about to go back to jail.

Zebra Finches are commonly kept as pets in this country. This one was a fugitive from a neighbor's house. She left after a half hour and never returned. Maybe one good taste of freedom was enough and she decided to go home, but it's more likely that she didn't survive.

You don't count escaped species as feeder birds because that would be cheating. Nor do you count peripheral species like the Golden-crowned Kinglet, which visit without eating any seeds or suet. Eastern Phoebe, Brown Creeper, Eastern Bluebird, American Robin, Northern Mockingbird, and a few warbler species come under this heading.

Phoebes have used the hanging feeders as perches from which to hawk insects. In April, a pair of bluebirds inspected the curtain feeder, eyeing the seeds suspiciously. They were confusing it with a birdhouse. The robin, state bird of Connecticut, has built a nest in the pine. I think the mockingbird visits now and then simply because it is curious about all the activity. The creeper and the warblers may have visited because of the presence of chickadees and titmice, which in the woods form the nucleus of mixed-species flocks.

Birds gain from joining mixed flocks because more eyes mean greater protection from predators. The flock, moreover, uncovers food sources more readily than an individual does, and since it comprises different species, there are fewer direct competitors than there are in a single-species flock of the same size. At the feeder, however, the increased foraging efficiency that mixed flocks enjoy in the woods probably evaporates. Insectivorous birds like creepers and warblers would seem to gain little from associating with chickadees and titmice that are concentrating on sunflower seeds. So, after checking out the feeder environs, such peripheral species move on.

The Gray Catbird used to be a peripheral species. Then one day I saw it fly into the pine and take a quick taste of suet. Maybe the catbird was after an ant crawling on the suet, but that would still make it a valid feeder species. By my rules, any wild bird the feeder nourishes, directly or indirectly, goes on the list.

My only other indirect, or collateral, species are Sharp-shinned, Cooper's, and Red-shouldered Hawks. The first two occur at the feeders with some regularity, and I'll get to them later. The Red-shouldered Hawk, however, was a onetime visitor.

Soon after I started feeding birds, a shrew moved into a space between the slates of my walkway. I'd watch it scoot out to grab seeds blown to the ground from one of the feeders. While it made one such foray, a Red-shouldered Hawk swooped in and landed in front of the door.

It was a fine-looking adult, and it stood less than eight feet away—no binoculars required. My wooded streamside location is good habitat for this fairly large buteo, whose varied diet includes small mammals, reptiles, amphibians, and birds. Recently, I saw one in the yard eating an earthworm, and there are reports of Red-shouldered Hawks coming to feeders for suet.

The hawk's length and wingspan approximate the crow's, but it weighs 40 percent more and in flight gives the impression of being closer in size to the larger Red-tailed Hawk. This one had flown in with remarkable speed, angling into the walkway with all the agility of an accipiter. With its chestnut shoulders, heavily banded tail, rufous underparts, and trim build, I rank the Red-shouldered as the East's handsomest buteo.

I was so taken with the hawk's surprise appearance that I had forgotten the shrew. It was locked in the grip of a raised talon. Before flying off, the hawk stood for a few seconds, squeezing. I regretted losing my tiny neighbor, but I couldn't fault the hawk. All predators should do their work so cleanly.

Blue Jays do a convincing imitation of the Red-shouldered Hawk's call, a descending *keeyer*, and they often make this sound at the feeder. Their mimicry seems designed to disconcert the other birds. Jays are full of bluster; they want it known that they are bigger, smarter, and more colorful than the rest.

To make their point, the jays arrive with a yell, flapping wildly. This sends other birds flying for cover in the higher branches of the pine. The startled birds resume feeding in moments, but the jays seem satisfied. They have commanded, however briefly, the same respect given a Sharp-shinned Hawk.

Compare this with the way crows approach, and you would never guess the two species belong to the same family. The crows land far from the house and walk the last 50 yards. They come with lowered heads, peering at the windows. If they detect the slightest movement, they're gone. To avoid coming any closer than necessary, they stretch to reach the seeds scattered around the pine. They hesitate before every bite because that is when they are most vulnerable. No feeder bird is smarter. In this respect they are closest to us, yet they want to stay as far away from us as possible.

The jays started coming in numbers only last winter, after a neighbor moved away. They had crowded to her feeder for leftover baked goods—muffins, crackers, bagels, pizza crust, cereal, bread—but her secret weapon was tortilla chips. "They're a Blue Jay magnet," she once told me. At present, I reserve such goodies for myself, but I would hate to lose the jays, so if they get bored with my pedestrian fare, or if a neighbor tries to lure them away, I'm prepared to share my tortilla chips. I'll even throw in larger portions of peanut kernels, and if need be, I'll sweeten the deal with gray-striped sunflower seeds.

Five or six jays come regularly. It's probably a family group consisting of parents with their young from last season. They prefer the tray feeder, where they fill their gullets with black-oil sunflower seeds (storing them, perhaps, in tree cavities), or take a single seed and move to a pine branch to hammer it open.

The jays gathered peacefully on the tray through winter, but at the first hints of spring they began stabbing at each other, and now, in early April, they usually come singly. I look forward to seeing them in August, when jays molt and lose all their head feathers at once. With their plucked gray skin, visible ear openings, oversize bill, and bulging eyes, they look like dinosaurs, or grotesque vultures.

In their molting attire, jays seem to lose their bravado, but at all other times they stand at the top of the feeder pecking order, though they are not alone. If a jay should find itself on the tray with a grackle, it's a standoff, and the other day a Red-bellied Woodpecker, though smaller than a jay, drove one away with a thrust of its formidable bill.

The Red-bellied Woodpecker is a subtle beauty, on a par with the grackle and the breeding-plumaged White-throated Sparrow. It made its first appearance while I was on the phone. Leaning back in my chair, I noticed a bird with salmon-colored underparts at the suet feeder. I promptly ended the call. This was the male I'd had been trying all winter to lure from my next-door neighbor's feeder.

Now a male and a female come almost every day—separately in winter, together in spring. In July they start bringing their young. I have watched a frazzled adult male feed a juvenile male and female in response to their wheezy begging calls. The siblings waited on a pine branch while the father fetched chunks of suet. The young male pecked at the female to drive her farther out on the branch, so he could monopolize the food. Although the female received only one good mouthful, she seemed capable of going to the suet herself if she got hungry enough.

Downy and Hairy Woodpeckers also visit with their young in early summer. One Downy father struck me as particularly devoted. He looked emaciated, and his worn plumage had a gray cast. Yet he repeatedly gathered suet treats for his two offspring, who waited on a branch above him. They were pictures of avian health—plump and brightly plumaged. If anyone in this family needed nurturing, it seemed to be the father. Luckily for him, young Downies are not dependent for long. Three weeks later, I saw the same adult male, assisted by his mate, chasing the two juveniles from the suet.

Parents disciplining their young, larger birds elbowing aside smaller ones, an occasional brawl between two members of the same species—such pecking-order skirmishes were virtually all my feeders saw of violence until a warm and drizzly January morning three years ago. I was sitting at my desk when a medium-size bird slammed into the glass door, leaving a circular mark of light dust about three inches in diameter, and a single down feather.

Earlier I had heard the whistling wings of Mourning Doves. I went to the door to investigate and flushed an accipiter from beneath the curtain feeder. It was either a female Sharp-shinned Hawk or a male Cooper's Hawk. I couldn't tell which because I was distracted by the Mourning Dove in the hawk's talons.

The hawk carried the dove to the woods lining the stream. Although the dove seemed a large load, the hawk flew without apparent effort. I couldn't see the hawk in the jumble of trees but knew it was there because crows flew in to mob it.

This is how I reconstruct the kill: The hawk locked onto the dove and flew in fast. The surprised dove instinctively tried to go in the opposite direction, but the door blocked its escape, and it hit the glass with great force. The collision, if not fatal, stunned the dove long enough for the hawk to grab it.

I can hear those whistling wings now. The dove had made it through weeks of cold, snow, and ice. It had just awakened from a rainy night and was looking for the day's first meal. It was pecking around the feeder pole for a few fallen seeds. But a hawk needs breakfast, too. After a few violent seconds everything was back to normal: songbirds in the pine, ducks and geese on the pond, my cat scratching to get out the door. I let the dusty mark on the glass stay as a memorial.

Three days later an immature Cooper's Hawk landed in front of the door. This was the dove killer. He was nearly crow size but slimmer, easily 16 inches long. He ran into the bushes below the curtain feeder and the small birds, mostly juncos, scattered.

I started noticing more accipiters—a Cooper's Hawk chasing a flock of starlings, another flying low and fast over the stream; a Sharp-shinned Hawk scanning bushes from a tree next to the driveway, a second sharpie being chased by jays (a risky enterprise). An innocence had left my backyard Eden. The lions had discovered the water hole. Ironically, I've seen more predation here—ten times more—than I have on all my walks in the woods.

This includes two more glass-related kills. In separate incidents, another Mourning Dove and a Tufted Titmouse were stunned after flying into my door. Each was scooped up by a Sharp-shinned Hawk. I've also had hawks fly into the glass when the bird they were chasing turned away at the last moment. Recently, a Sharpie and an unidentified songbird hit the glass almost simultaneously.

At first I thought this was an accipiter hunting technique. The hawks seemed to be driving prey into the glass intentionally. When the hawks themselves started hitting, I realized that the collisions were probably accidents. The hawks follow their targeted birds very closely. The fleeing birds hit more often because they are in front. If the impact stuns them, the hawks are only too glad to take advantage of the situation. But if the hawks can't stop in time, they become victims, too.

What about the decals on my glass door? In the heat of the chase, prey and predator alike hit the door despite them. The fleeing birds, so desperate to get away, probably don't notice the decals, and the hawks don't notice because they're focused on the fleeing birds. To make the glass more obvious, this spring I doubled the number of decals. When accipiters return in the fall, I'll learn how well this corrective measure works.

Other people who feed birds may complain about the jay-size Sharpie and the larger Cooper's, relatives of the Northern

Goshawk. When I lived in Weston, the local newspaper had a bird column that answered reader questions. A man wanted advice on dealing with a marauding Sharpie. "They're killing my birds," he wrote.

They're not his birds, of course, and since predation is natural, there's no problem to solve. Am I setting up the birds by feeding them? Their constant wariness proves to me that they're perfectly aware of the danger, yet they choose to come anyway, just as the gazelle comes to the water hole knowing the lion may lie in wait. Sharp-shinned and Cooper's Hawks, moreover, are protected by law, and most people who feed birds never see them.

I can't say that their presence thrills me. I am, however, awed by them. In my view their predatory powers far exceed those of the lion, which gorges itself on a kill and may go days before making another. Sharp-shinned and Cooper's Hawks don't have the luxury of so much time. Relative to their size, their metabolic demands are much greater, so they must hunt much more frequently.

The Sharpie, for example, must kill approximately one bird a day to survive. If it misses a day, or suffers an injury that impairs its hunting ability only slightly, it is in serious trouble. It does not hunt cooperatively, like the lion. It has no choice but to be self-reliant. This predator, in short, knows what it means to feel pressure. Have sympathy, then, for the Sharpie when you hear a story like the following.

It begins at 5:15 p.m. on January 28. I had just scattered seeds on the ground for the cardinals, which always feed just before dark. A female was out there, chipping at the other cardinals to keep them away from her feeding space near the trunk of the pine. I needed something from the closet near the front door but didn't want to flush her, so I took the long way around the room, ducking behind things. I wish I had flushed her. I wish I had sent her to her roost a little hungry.

Her chipping turned more rapid and urgent. When I looked out, she was still on the ground next to the pine trunk, but with a female sharp-shinned hawk on her back. The hawk must have come up behind her while she was distracted with protecting her space from the other cardinals, none of whom were in sight. It was a terribly swift and stunningly successful surprise attack.

The hawk had sunk her talons into the cardinal's back and was rocking quickly to drive them deeper, with an expression that I can only describe as fiendish. The cardinal called feebly. She was pinned down, unable to move a muscle, in the same position as when I had first seen her. Only a few seconds had passed—maybe the pain hadn't registered.

While the cardinal sat there, still alive and fully awake, the hawk began plucking feathers from her breast. After a few plucks the cardinal jerked her head perpendicular to her body and closed her eyes—her death throe. I had been waiting for the hawk to finish off the cardinal by biting her neck, but that's a falcon's killing method, not an accipiter's.

The Sharpie spared me further horror by spiriting the cardinal away—across the lawn and into the woods—but what nightmarish images she left behind! Yes, I was tempted to intervene, but I held back because I knew the cardinal was fatally wounded from the start. Had I rushed out to save her, I would have only prolonged her agony, and how could I justify taking away the hawk's kill? Better that I should take away this sobering lesson: The Sharp-shinned Hawk hunts in gathering dusk and respects neither the cardinal's beauty nor the nature writer's sensibilities.

The deadly game goes on. A Cooper's Hawk flies into the pine and perches briefly on the limb closest to the house. The songbirds escape, but the hawk hops around the branches looking for a straggler. I step out to look and the hawk stays—bold, I think.

A Sharpie buzzes Mourning Doves perched in trees along the stream, then it buzzes the feeder. A Blue Jay calls repeatedly and moves deeper into the pine; a Red-bellied Woodpecker whips around to the far side of the pine trunk. The hawk returns to the trees, flying erratically as if trying to cause a panic and force a potential victim into the open.

Mourning Doves feeding under the pine explode into the air, telling me something's up. In a moment a Cooper's Hawk flies in casually, testing them, perhaps. Later, he makes a more serious pass at Tufted Titmice on the sunflower tube feeder, but he comes up empty. The titmice escape into the thick pine foliage, giving their high, repeated alarm call, one of the best tip-offs that a hawk is around.

Another tip-off: when birds freeze in place. They'll sit on a feeder perch or on a pine branch, or they'll cling to the pine trunk, and the only movement you'll see is the blink of their nictitating membrane. They've spotted a hawk and don't want to give themselves away.

The hawk may lose that opportunity, but it will be back. In a steady rain on a late September morning, a female Sharp-shinned Hawk snatched an immature Downy Woodpecker from the suet feeder. The hawk fluttered up from below and, in an upside-down position, picked off the Downy from the bottom of the suet cage.

No one saw it coming. Chickadees, titmice, goldfinches, and House Finches shot away from the other feeders. The Downy screamed repeatedly but briefly, only until the hawk landed with it on the walkway. The hawk calmly waited for the struggling Downy to die, giving it an occasional thrust of the talons before flying off with it. She had none of the cardinal-killing Sharpie's fiendishness.

As kills go, it was matter-of-fact, but as sad for me as the death of the cardinal had been. I knew this juvenile Downy, though I'm not sure whether it was male or female. At a young age, the sexes look alike. The Downy had been coming to the feeders since fledging. Its first visits were with its father. On that fateful morning, I had noticed how drenched it was. The chickadees and titmice returned in 15 minutes and fed as if nothing had happened. They were reasonably safe from Sharpie attacks, but only for the rest of that day.

The accipiters that stake out my feeder usually attack from a distance. Last winter, however, a different tactic surfaced. After rushing a small flock of chickadees and titmice, which escaped into the woods, a female Sharpie hunkered in the pine. I went out and found her perched quietly near the treetop. She allowed me a close approach, though she peered at me suspiciously and craned her neck to keep me in view.

She sat there half an hour. The chickadees and titmice returned and, judging by their vigorous calling, knew she was there. More birds followed: two Downies, two White-breasted Nuthatches, and several House Sparrows. The hawk stayed put, perhaps waiting for a bird to come within reach. As I mulled over the ethics of flushing her, the Downies zoomed away in alarm. I checked the pine—no hawk, and no sign of a kill.

Three days later, the same hawk landed in the pine during a snowstorm. Some birds flew away, others stayed. The hawk moved about the branches just above the feeders, looking up at the stragglers, who departed one by one. She eventually disappeared into the pine's upper reaches. Fifteen minutes later, as a chickadee and a titmouse perched on the sunflower tube feeder, the hawk plummeted toward them. On the way, she hit a branch and sent the snow spraying, a lucky break for the chickadee and titmouse. I felt the hawk's humiliation. But an accipiter cannot bat a thousand. The best of them are .300 hitters.

One immature male Cooper's Hawk, however, had a much lower batting average. I called him the comical Cooper's Hawk because, after striking out, he'd stand in front of the door with the most baffled expression. Then he'd run into one end of the row of bushes against the house, and the sparrows would run out the other.

Of course, he must have connected often enough, but I worried about him, especially when he showed up one day at the tail end of a blizzard. He attacked with reckless abandon but, as usual, he missed. For a moment he perched on the tray feeder. It was getting dark, and in his wild eyes I saw desperation. He'd have to get through the night on an empty stomach. In the morning he'd be weak, yet under even greater pressure to kill.

He pulled through somehow: Four days later, he returned. And what's this? He landed in the pine clutching a small bird. I strained to see whether it was one of my favorites. Because there was brown on its back, I feared it was a Carolina Wren. But no, it was just a House Sparrow, a male snatched from the flock that frequents the tangles at the edge of the pond.

With the sparrow in its vicelike grip, the hawk waited several minutes, yet the sparrow was still alive and struggling when the plucking began. By the time most birds would have been dead, the sparrow repeatedly tried to bite. The hawk responded to these outbursts by pulling his head a safe distance away, partly to avoid injury—and partly, it seemed, out of respect for the sparrow's fighting spirit.

When the sparrow finally stopped moving, the hawk plucked in earnest, letting the feathers fall to the ground. The wing feathers required the most strenuous yanking. Never before had I seen the entire process of an accipiter devouring its kill. Starting with the head, the hawk tore into the sparrow, gulping flesh and bone.

While the hawk fed, a Tufted Titmouse came to the sunflower tube feeder. It slowly raised and lowered its crest, which I took as a sure sign that it saw the hawk. Just as the zebra can read the difference between a satiated lion and a hungry one, the titmouse can read when a hawk isn't on the hunt.

In 15 minutes all that remained of the sparrow was the pile of feathers under the pine. The hawk cleaned his bill—vigorously rubbing each side against a branch—sat upright, pulled one bloody talon into his belly, and balanced on the other. It was a short nap. A squirrel climbed the pine, apparently looking to scavenge, and the hawk flew.

I had new respect for the Cooper's Hawk—he was no longer comical—and new respect for his victim, who fought long after there was no hope. What powerful evidence of a wild animal's will to live! The phrase "just a House Sparrow" has been removed from my vocabulary.

Looking at my feeders on a quiet summer day, I can hardly believe so much has happened around them. I regret that I didn't start feeding birds sooner. During my intermediate birding years I scoffed at feeding. It was too suburban an activity, I thought, pursued by many people who don't consider themselves birders.

Some of them don't even care to know the common names of the birds they feed. Such a fraternity wasn't for me.

I paid the price of snobbery by missing so much in those years. Now when I drive past a house with filled bird feeders, I feel differently. No matter that the people inside might call American Goldfinches "those adorable little yellow-and-black ones." I feel a kinship with such people. We probably share the belief that no place would be home without bird feeders, that feeders are as integral to the home landscape as flower boxes. Bird feeding done right is one of the great pleasures of suburban living—of living anywhere. Why would anyone not want to feed the birds?

CHAPTER 9

SPIRIT PLACES

It is not down on any map;
true places never are.
HERMAN MELVILLE

PART OF THE CHARM OF SOUTHERN NEW ENGLAND IS THAT DISTINCTIVE features of the landscape often occur on a human scale. Subtle in their appeal and sometimes hidden, these special places may not be readily noticed.

A seasonal waterfall in Newtown's Lower Paugusset State Forest is a perfect example. I passed within a minute's walk of it a dozen times without suspecting it existed. How could someone who likes to think of himself as observant be guilty of such an over-sight? I can only plead that there were many distractions.

The main trail in this thousand-acre forest follows Lake Zoar, a dammed section of the Housatonic River, and threads its way through woods dominated by hemlocks that rise straight and tall from steep riverside slopes. In places, pure stands of hemlocks unfold into the distance, and some of the trees are giants. Walking among them on a summer day, you might hear the diaphanous song of a Hermit Thrush—if the motorboats buzzing up and down the river don't drown out the bird's voice.

The stately trees, the rhythm of walking, the undulations of the trail, and the periodic views of the wide, slow river set between rolling hills usually lull me into a wilderness reverie. I now realize that you can hear the waterfall as you approach Prydden Brook, a mile and a half from the trailhead, but time after time I must have thought the sound was the wind, if I heard it at all.

Then one day I came to the languid brook and stopped. Instead of crossing, I wandered along it toward the river, going around a bend. Finally I became conscious of a low but unmistakable roar. Stepping over the thickly needled sprays of fallen hemlock branches, I found myself at the top of the waterfall.

It tumbled below me for about 50 feet over a series of broad step-like rocks. Catching its excitement, I scrambled to the bottom. There I concluded that this was about the finest little waterfall I had ever found.

No artist, I thought, could conjure up the picture that nature had hung on this riverside slope. The brook threw itself down the rocks in long frothy sheets, splashy buckets, and pencil-thin streams. Moss-covered rocks and a fallen timber, glistening wet, filled the spaces. Silvery green hemlocks arched above the commotion. From a fern-fringed pool at the bottom of the waterfall, the brook resumed its winding course toward the Housatonic. A hundred yards away it blended into the river with barely a ripple.

I returned to the top and worked my way back down, noting how abruptly the water changed character. Just above the waterfall, the brook was calm—almost stagnant—and only inches deep. When it came spilling down the rocks, not only did it flow faster; it also seemed to grow in volume, as if fed by some magical spring.

A true waterfall plummets from a considerable height in a great display of earthshaking power, bathing nearby admirers in benevolent spray. This was falling water of a lesser magnitude—showy rather than awesome. Standing only yards away, I felt none of its wetness. Whatever it lacked in grandeur, though, it made up for in approachable New England beauty. This humble natural wonder may have a name, but I dubbed it One Man's Cascade. Its intimate scale seemed to dictate that it be viewed alone.

Although I had been coming to the forest for a year before stumbling upon the cascade, the thrill of discovery was worth the wait, and I was grateful no one had told me about it. Clearly it was no secret. Nearby, an open area had the well-worn look of a picnic ground, bicycle tracks tore across a slope, and there were No Camping signs, riddled with gunshots, on some of the trees.

Some weeks later, I was approaching the cascade on an unmarked side trail when I spied three people and a dog clambering among its rocks. Would I be a proper social animal and join them? No. The spell would be broken. Ascending a slope, I picked up the main trail and followed the brook in the opposite direction—feeling a little cheated, debating with myself whether to turn back. The hemlocks thinned out, giving way to sunlight and open deciduous woods, with mountain laurels lining the brook.

No one, it seemed, had passed through this placid scenery lately. As if to confirm my feeling, a pair of Mallard burst up from an island in the brook. They flew high above the trees, and I lost them behind a hill. Soon they were circling back, telling me they probably had a nest. So I moved on—happy to leave them to their parental duties, and reassured that, wherever one decides to go, discoveries await.

WHEN YOU CROSS THE POWER LINE ON THE TRAIL TO MOHAWK STATE Forest's black spruce bog, it is like crossing to the wild's other side. You plunge from light into deep shade; from open, mixed woods into a stand of old evergreens. Suddenly the forest emits a supernatural aura. On the right a hemlock's gnarled roots grip a boulder, and a pink glow surrounds the branchless trunks of a group of red pines. The trail dips, and ahead the canopy opens slightly. A lumpy carpet of moss and a twisting boardwalk mark the beginning of the bog.

Rare in Connecticut, the black spruce bog is a type of forested wetlands. In my part of the country, it occurs most frequently in northern New York and northern New England. This bog, ensconced in cool, wooded highlands, is about 50 miles north of Danbury, at the end of a 550-foot trail. I went to the bog three times one summer, seduced by its unfamiliar plants, Adirondack atmosphere, accessibility, and oozing wetness. It covers a mere two acres, and after going 150 feet across the sphagnum moss, the boardwalk stops. Still, there is enough here to occupy the curious naturalist or mystic seeker for hours.

The bog is believed to have formed in a watery depression, or kettle hole, left by a block of ice after the last glacial period. Generations of sphagnum moss lived and died in the water, gradually filling the kettle hole from the edges inward with peat, a blackish muck. An accumulation of peat 40 feet deep, completely covered by living moss, lurks below the boardwalk. In what might be thought of as the classic bog, a quaking mat of floating sphagnum moss, largely free of other vegetation, surrounds open water. Here, in contrast, trees and shrubs that can live in the bog's wet, acidic, nutrient-poor soil grow across the full extent of the moss, dominated by black spruces that reach a height of 50 feet. Impenetrable clusters of young spruces fringe the end of the boardwalk.

The black spruce shares the bog with another northern tree, the lovely tamarack. Also known as the American larch, the tamarack is the only deciduous conifer native to the Northeast. Tamarack needles grow in soft brushlike clumps and turn from blue-green to yellow before dropping in the fall. Highbush blueberry and mountain holly crowd the bog's understory; sheep laurel grows just above the moss

The bog's catalog of botanical curiosities includes the carnivorous pitcher plant. Insects crawl down its steep sides, past downward-pointing fibers. They come to a smooth area where the plant's lining sticks to their feet and makes them lose traction. Unable to climb out, the insects slip to the base of the plant, into a mixture of rainwater and digestive juices.

Sphagnum moss can absorb 20 times its weight in water, so the wetness that defines the bog may not always be evident. One cloudy afternoon, I learned this the hard way. When I stepped off the end of the boardwalk onto ground that I mistook for a continuation of the trail, I sank to my ankles.

I turned back and sat cross-legged on the planks. Songs of summering birds wafted across the spongy terrain, including a Dark-eyed Junco, Black-throated Blue Warblers, a Blue-headed Vireo, and a host of Hermit Thrushes—all species with a northern affinity. In the dense vegetation, the only bird I saw was a Northern Waterthrush.

The sky grew darker, and thunder rumbled in the distance. Hunkered in this gothic greenery, I fell into a boggy mood. Past and present, living and dead, real and unreal seem to mingle in the bog. It was easy to envision a civilization of bog dwellers roaming below me through torchlit halls of mud. If I waited long enough, maybe I would glimpse their nightly foray into the upper world. The bog would have none of it. The thunder was getting louder, and raindrops had coated the boardwalk. I left this spirit place to its rightful owners.

The remnants of Dudleytown, my last spirit place, lie nearby—on a hill in the village of Cornwall Bridge. Settled in the mid-1700s, Dudleytown was all but abandoned by the early 1900s. Today, stone foundations and cellar holes, surrounded by New England's ubiquitous stone walls, stand as solemn memorials to the small, troubled community that once existed there. Rocky soil and cold winters—banes of the New England farmer—have been blamed for Dudleytown's demise. But a legend has grown up with the thick forest that now covers the once pastoral landscape: From the start, Dudleytown was cursed.

The curse has been traced to an English nobleman, ancestor of the Dudley brothers who settled the town. Back in England, old Edmund Dudley got his head chopped off for plotting against King Henry VII. Someone or something put a curse on Edmund that followed his family to the New World and took root in Dudleytown. How else to explain the disproportionate number of horrors that befell tiny Dudleytown's residents? According to some local historians, the town's stony remains have witnessed madness, suicide, fatal accidents, natural disasters, and vanishings.

In what is often cited as the first manifestation of the curse, one of the Dudley brothers went insane. A string of other strange incidents followed: At a barn raising, a man fell to his death (or was it murder?). Lightning struck and killed a Dudleytown wife, right on her porch. A sheepherder watched helplessly as the curse destroyed his family. His wife died of tuberculosis, and his children disappeared. When his house burned down, he wandered into the woods, never to return. According to the chroniclers of Dudleytown, *New York Tribune* editor Horace Greeley should have followed his own advice ("Go West, young man") and taken his wife. They claim that Mrs. Greeley, otherwise known as Mary Cheney, hanged herself in Dudleytown in 1872.

It should be noted that Rev. Gary P. Dudley, a Texas resident and the author of *The Legend of Dudleytown: Solving Legends Through Genealogical and Historical Research*, disputes the foregoing. In tracing the genealogy of his name, he found virtually no historical basis for Dudleytown's cursed reputation—no genealogical link to Edmund Dudley, no mysterious illnesses or deaths. As for Mary Cheney, he says she never set foot in Dudleytown.

By most accounts, including Mr. Dudley's, the final resident of Dudleytown was William Clarke, a New York City physician. Dr. Clarke built a vacation home in Dudleytown in the early 1900s. Mrs. Clarke was yet another wife visited by tragedy. The traditional story places her in Dudleytown at the time. While her husband attended to an emergency in the city, leaving her alone overnight, she descended into madness. (As Dudley tells it, Mrs. Clarke committed suicide—in New York, not in Dudleytown.) Before moving out of Dudleytown, Dr. Clarke founded Dark Entry Forest, Inc., an association of property owners that designated Dudleytown a nature preserve. As Dudleytown fell to ruin, the land reverted to forest.

The locals avoid Dudleytown, and according to legend, so do wild animals. Except for the owls. In the ever present darkness that shrouds Dudleytown Hill, owls are said to hoot throughout the day. Hence Dudleytown's nickname: Owlsbury.

One soggy afternoon in mid-October, I decided to investigate Dudleytown. Following directions in a guide to nature walks in Connecticut, I drove with a slightly reluctant companion to the 750-acre preserve's main entrance at the end of Bald Mountain Road in Cornwall Bridge. There we saw something frightful indeed: a slew of No Parking and No Trespassing signs in front of a locked gate.

As we assessed the situation, an SUV came barreling down a nearby driveway. Out jumped a woman who warned that if we dared park there, someone would photograph my car and call the police. Before disappearing down the street, she raised the specter of towing, fines, and arrest.

When we got over the shock, I took out my maps and saw that we could enter Dudleytown from the Mohawk Trail, a bit farther north. From there it's a 1.5-mile hike to Dudleytown, but with our false start we wouldn't get there until after dark. I wanted to experience Dudleytown at night, but I'd planned to see it in daylight as well. We agreed to return the following weekend.

Meanwhile, I did some digging and learned why Dudleytown's neighbors don't cotton to strangers. The legend has long attracted paranormal investigators, journalists, hikers, the occasional birder, curiosity seekers, and just plain folk inclined toward the supernatural. But in 1999, after the release of *The Blair Witch Project* (the hugely popular movie about haunted woods in Maryland), goings on at Dudleytown got out of hand. Web sites, meanwhile, were spreading the legend far beyond its traditional word-of-mouth audience.

Complaining of drinking parties, campfires, littering, disorderly conduct, and vandalism, the members of Dark Entry Forest, Inc., placed Dudleytown off-limits. A press release they sent to local papers noted that, in a single year, police had been called to the area 79 times. One case involved five teenagers who got lost in Dudleytown at 1:30 a.m. They used a cell phone to call 911, and the police dispatched a search team that included state troopers, firefighters, dogs, and a helicopter. While conducting their rescue, the team scared up a separate group of six teenagers. Each trespasser was fined $77.

Such high jinks explain why a sign in the Mohawk Trail parking lot warns hikers to keep out from October 25 to November 4. The trail crosses Dark Entry Forest land, including a corner of Dudleytown. In deference to the neighbors, the Connecticut Forest and Park Association closes this leg of the trail for several days on either side of Halloween. Straying from the Dudleytown section of the trail at any time of year may constitute trespassing. The only way to enter the heart of Dudleytown legally is to obtain a pass from Dark Entry Forest, Inc.

We pulled into the lot on the afternoon of October 20. It was sunny and cool, and come evening, we'd see a nearly full moon. Driving north on Route 7, I had marveled at the fabled Litchfield Hills in their autumn colors and at the crowds of tourists on Main Street in Kent.

The blue blazes of the Mohawk Trail follow Dark Entry Road, which climbs steeply and passes several houses and many towering trees—including one with a bulging, fistlike trunk—before narrowing into a hiking path that hugs Bonney Brook. As we trudged along the road, Golden-crowned Kinglets flitted about the treetops, their energetic three-note calls punctuating our breathless conversation. We saw a Myrtle Warbler and two or three Hermit Thrushes; heard a Pileated Woodpecker, chickadees, titmice, and nuthatches. The birds gave no signal that we should abort our mission.

After plunging into the forest, we passed a huge fallen hemlock rotting away on the opposite bank of Bonney Brook, its red carcass folded over blackish rocks. Soon we reached a broken stone wall that crosses the brook. Once it had been a dam—Witches' Dam, some now call it. Nearby, we heard a hollow moaning that we traced to a thin stream of water spouting into a rocky pool.

A half mile beyond, we crossed the brook and entered Dudleytown, which the trail guide of the Connecticut Forest and Park Association refers to only as "an abandoned community." By then we were far from major roads. It was so quiet we spoke in hushed tones as we poked around the doomed settlement's stone ruins. Yet we still heard kinglets.

We weren't alone: Loud voices, startling in the sylvan silence, preceded the appearance of two young couples. I think we gave them a start, too, standing there calmly as they came around a turn in the trail.

They expressed interest in spirits and, noticing my binoculars, asked if I had seen any birds. They found it hard to believe I had, even after I pointed out a Hairy Woodpecker over their shoulders. Apparently they subscribed to the "wild animals shun Dudleytown" part of the legend. Intent on getting out of Dudleytown before dark, they moved on.

Although the trail closes at sunset, we stretched the rules and stayed until dark to get the full effect. Some have experienced vortexes and cold spots in Dudleytown. Others have seen apparitions or recorded them on film (though cameras and other battery-powered equipment don't always work there). A few claim to have been chased, even slapped, by ghosts. My friend and I cannot count ourselves among the chosen few.

Still, I was impressed that Dudleytown lived up to its nickname. We did hear owls in Owlsbury—a late afternoon love duet performed by male and female Barred Owls. Almost simultaneously, we heard the croaks of two Common Ravens—Edgar Allan Poe's "ghastly grim and ancient" wanderers. They passed directly over us, cackling to each other as they flew to night's Plutonian shore.

On the way out, we made some wrong turns but never strayed far from the trail—with a little backtracking, we picked it up again. Flying squirrels squeaked in the moonlight; a Canada Goose honked. I pretended that the blue trail blazes painted on the trees had turned scarlet and dripping wet in the darkness. "Shut up," said my friend.

We heard distant wailing—maybe a coyote—and in the gloom of Dark Entry Road, my friend almost stepped on a junco, which had been lying on its side. It fluttered up and disappeared into hemlock saplings. Had it become intoxicated from feasting on fermented berries? Was it a tired migrant? Or had it succumbed to Dudleytown's spell?

CHAPTER 10

NUMBERS

IN MAY, AS THE SPRING MIGRATION OF BIRDS PEAKS ACROSS MUCH OF North America, hard-core birders compete in one or more Big Day, or "birdathon," counts. The object of a Big Day is to see as many species as possible within a 24-hour period. When the goal is at least a hundred species, a Big Day is known as a Century Run. The most competitive birders chase relentlessly after species that will augment their lists, a level of intensity that may not be altogether healthy. Roger Tory Peterson, himself a Big Day participant, in his early field guides distanced himself from the "grim grind" of such marathoners.

I am not a numbers person, but since counts are something of a tradition in birding, I've participated in my share—mostly Big Day and Christmas counts. The vast majority were grim grinds indeed. A few, however, kindled my competitive spirit. The northward movement of birds that begins as a trickle in mid-February reached a particularly notable flood stage one May 11. For another birder and me, it was our best ever Big Day count at Sherwood Island State Park.

We had done the count there for several years, confining our-selves to the 234-acre park and an adjacent tidal pond. Sherwood Island has woods, meadows, and thickets ringed by salt marshes, beaches, and tidal waters. These diverse coastal habitats, all within a compact area, account for the park's bird checklist of some 285 species. This is the total number of bird species ever recorded in the park. With favorable weather a birder can see close to a third of them on a May morning.

On that May 11, as we got out of our cars at 6:30 a.m. on the wooded peninsula where we always began our Big Days, the musi-cal din of bird sounds told us something special was happening. It was fair and warm, with a light southwest wind, the best weather for spring birding by our experience. We began checking off species in quick succession and soon realized this was the day we had been hoping for. With the birds singing all around us, we turned to each other and agreed we were going to hit a hundred.

Any bird you see on land, in the air, or on the water goes onto your Big Day list. We scoured the park's woods for songbirds; slogged through marsh mud to find waders and shorebirds; strained our eyes looking for waterfowl on the sound and the tidal pond—at high and low tides. By the end of the day I suffered from "warbler neck," a malady that comes from staring into the tree-tops for hours.

Our expectations were borne out. There were so many birds in the park that by the time we broke for lunch at nearby Sherwood Diner, we had amassed 101 species. Some years it was hard enough to break the 90-species mark, and getting those last few birds is the tough part. On this day it had been easy. In places, land birds streamed through the trees or spilled across our path. Waterbirds rushed over the island in sporadic waves. Most birds, however, came through in spurts. We had to be quick in identifying them, because one brief look was often all we got.

After lunch we were poised to break our record of 104 species, which we had set two years earlier. When we emerged from the diner, however, the wind began to shift and soon came from the northwest, an unfavorable direction. The park, so alive with birds all morning, by afternoon became a different place. We went for long periods without seeing even common species, which dulled the edge of my identification skills. What kept us going was a pleasant daydream: only four more birds between us and glory. With seven hours of daylight left, I knew we would make it, but I was getting greedy. I was no longer content merely to break our record. I wanted to shatter it.

At 6:30, an electrical storm forced us from the east marsh back to our cars and prevented us from looking for the birds that come out at twilight: rail and owls. But by then we had done it. Thunder and lightning, nature's drum roll and fireworks, heralded our feat. Our new personal record for a Sherwood Island Big Day: 114 species, a ten-bird leap beyond our old mark. Of this combined total, I had 113 species and my friend had 112. He missed my Wood Ducks and Blue-gray Gnatcatcher; I missed his Northern Waterthrush. I heard seven species that I did not see but they counted, too. The songs and calls of most birds are vocal fingerprints, a means of identifying hidden species with absolute certainty.

Considering how many birds we counted, we were surprised to find only two rarities: a striking breeding-plumaged Tricolored Heron and an American Bittern. The day before, there had been two rare Red-necked Grebes on the sound, but on count day they disappeared. We knew there were Clapper Rail in the park, but they kept hidden, an even bigger disappointment. No Big Day is without a few frustrating misses.

Our hundredth species of the day was a flock of Glossy Ibises, uncommon at Sherwood Island. Number 114 was a Prairie Warbler that posed on a bush for a second, one of 16 warbler species. It took me until 4:30 to find a lone Rock Dove, also known as the Domestic Pigeon.

Our only raptor was a Red-tailed Hawk. There were 70 passerine, or perching, birds and 44 nonpasserines, which are mostly waterbirds. We birded the last two hours of the day without adding any species.

We saw almost 1,500 individual birds, the most numerous being Canada Goose (300), Double-crested Cormorant (200), Herring Gull (60), European Starling (50), and Red-winged Blackbird and Common Grackle (40 each). We were pleased to see 20 Least Terns—a threatened species in Connecticut, they nest on a nearby island and fish along the park's shoreline. Twenty-two species were represented by a single individual.

Blessedly, the lawn mowers were idle that day, and the park was nearly empty of people. In the spruce grove where we sometimes find wintering owls, we locked gazes with a coyote being mobbed by crows. It was probably on the prowl for woodchucks. There were few mosquitoes, but I was plagued all day by dog ticks. I flicked off 15 to 20 while we were birding and when I got home removed 25 from my clothes.

I crowed for months about our 114-species Big Day because the area we cover is small. Though it took us 12 hours to find that many birds, a person walking briskly could cross Sherwood

Island at its widest point in about 30 minutes. Will I ever again see that many birds at Sherwood Island? Are 125 or more birds possible? With many species of birds thought to be declining because of habitat loss and fragmentation of existing habitat, I'm skeptical. Despite our one-day success, in recent years the height of the spring migration has at times seemed disturbingly quiet. Like birds that once blanketed the sky, our record is receding into the past.

The end of the spring migration ushers in another count. In June, as the nesting season of birds shifts into high gear across much of the United States and Canada, a small army of birders hits the road to conduct the North American Breeding Bird Survey. Beginning a half hour before sunrise to catch the day's most intense period of bird song, they drive assigned 24.5-mile routes along secondary roads. At half-mile intervals they stop and count the birds they see or hear within a radius of a quarter mile. Each of some 3,000 survey routes covered each year requires 50 stops and takes about five hours to complete.

The U.S. Geological Survey's Patuxent Wildlife Research Center oversees the Breeding Bird Survey from its Laurel, Maryland, headquarters. BBS methodology has its limitations. Roadside observations do not adequately measure population trends for endangered and nocturnal birds, or for those that nest in colonies. Moreover, sections of road that pass natural areas—including the strips of vegetation often left as buffers between the road and cleared land—can give false impressions. Species may be common along these sections but absent in nearby areas where habitat has been destroyed.

Despite the "roadside bias" issue, the more than 30 years of BBS data collectively provides valuable insight into state, regional, and continental population trends of about 500 species of North American birds. BBS results have helped focus public attention on worrisome changes in bird populations, such as the decline of the Cerulean Warbler, the Eastern Towhee, the Red-headed Woodpecker, and the grassland birds east of the Mississippi River.

The news isn't all bad. Eastern Bluebird numbers, for example, increased more than 3 percent a year between 1980 and 2002, according to the BBS. The decline of this species, which nests in old woodpecker holes and in tree cavities formed by natural decay, was noted long before the first multistate BBS in 1966. Eastern Bluebirds thrive in sparsely wooded habitats: forest clearings, beaver ponds, meadows, and farmland. To feed, they fly from perches and catch insects on or near the ground. They often nest in dead, isolated trees.

At Sherwood Island I once found bluebirds nesting in a rotting white birch stump at the edge of a wooded knoll. The cavity was about four feet above the ground. From late May on, I returned to the site only once or twice a week, yet in one of the happiest coincidences of my birding career, I was there to witness the four bluebird fledglings leave the nest.

Each fledgling stuck its head out of the nest hole a few times before making the leap into the outside world. From surrounding trees the parents made soft, coaxing calls. The fledglings responded with sweet notes of their own. When one fledgling flew from the cavity, the head of the next appeared. In a matter of minutes, three of the fledglings were sitting on the same limb, high above the stump. The parents joined them, as the fourth fledgling watched from a nearby tree. I'd be hard-pressed to recall a more touching family picture.

The bluebird's decline began early in the 20th century, when the open habitats it requires were reverting to forest. Meanwhile, commercial and residential developers, and managers of timberlands, were removing the bluebird's existing nest sites. Dead trees were regarded as unsightly, and their wildlife value wasn't appreciated. Competition from the House Sparrow and the starling—aggressive cavity nesters introduced from Europe in the 1800s—and pesticide poisoning in the 1950s and 1960s worsened the bluebird's plight.

As far back as the 1930s, the bluebird's early advocates were promoting "bluebird trails"—a series of nest boxes weaving through appropriate habitat—but it wasn't until the 1970s that bluebird restoration on a massive scale took hold. Today, the North American Bluebird Society—dedicated to helping Eastern, Western, and Mountain Bluebirds, as well as other native cavity nesters—has several thousand members, and its Transcontinental Bluebird Trail comprises more than 20,000 nest boxes.

A number of state and provincial bluebird societies have sprung up as well, and on the Internet there is the Birdhouse Network, a nest box-monitoring project of the Cornell Laboratory of Ornithology. The Birdhouse Network maintains data on more than 30 species of cavity nesters, displays pictures from nest box cameras, and sponsors "citizen science" research. Like BBS volunteers, Bluebird Society members and Birdhouse Network participants are especially busy in June, monitoring nest boxes at the height of the breeding season.

More than 100,000 nest boxes are sold annually, and do-it-yourselfers build countless others. Eastern Bluebirds have also benefited in recent decades from the comeback of the beaver, which builds dams that flood riparian woodlands. Beaver ponds often contain dead, hole-ridden trees.

I've learned that installing a bluebird nest box is not a project to take lightly. You don't just nail a nest box to a tree and forget about it—that would be tantamount to serving predators a bluebird platter. If your nest box doesn't meet specifications, if it's not a safe haven, if you choose the wrong site, and if you don't monitor the box for problems, birds are far less likely to survive and to nest successfully, if any move in. *The Bluebird Monitor's Guide* and *The Backyard Birdhouse Book* steered me in the right direction.

Aside from commitment, an avian housing program may require a significant outlay of cash, especially if you're mechanically challenged like I am. For my store-bought bluebird nest box, metal mounting pole, stovepipe-style raccoon guard, and attachment hardware, I paid over $90—more than three times what Thoreau paid to construct his cabin on Walden Pond. My building materials, furthermore, were harder to find.

Just put yourself in a cavity nester's place, and you'll see justification for all the precautions. When you're seven inches long and weigh little more than an ounce, the placid suburb is fraught with dangers: domestic cats, raccoons and other wild carnivores, hawks, nest-robbing birds such as jays and crows, squirrels, snakes, wasps, blood-sucking flies, competing cavity nesters, and human vandals. Holed up in a wooden chamber, your one escape route is likely to be blocked by the predator that has come to eat you. Contaminated waterways, noise pollution, and pesticides pose additional threats.

Of course, predation, accidents, and disease are natural in the wild, and if you spend time helping wildlife, you're bound to experience tragic losses, as I did in early May of last year. My nest box attracted a Tree Swallow—a species that often uses boxes designed for bluebirds. The swallow spent most of two days resting inside the box, which overlooks the stream-fed pond in my back-yard. Once, when I opened the box's hinged front panel, the swallow flew out, skimmed the surface of the pond for a drink, and circled higher to catch flying insects. I decided the bird was okay, perhaps waiting for the arrival of a mate, but when I checked the box on the third day, the swallow lay dead inside, with no visible injuries.

The mysterious circumstances of the death disturbed me but gave me no reason to abandon my project. After cleaning the box I put it back up, and though bluebirds inspected it, this time a pair of Tree Swallows moved in. Tree Swallows seem less common in my neighborhood than bluebirds, so I was thrilled.

While the female swallow was in the box, brooding the clutch of eggs in her feather-lined nest, the male often stood guard on a snag curving over the pond. Sometimes they zoomed around together, showing their incredible flying skill as they picked off insects. If my curiosity brought me too close to the nest box when the protective female was outside, she dove at me while calling angrily.

When her eggs hatched she became even more aggressive and defended a larger area. Once she came at me as I stood at the edge of the pond, a good 75 yards from the nest box. Almost grazing the top of my head, she let out a *"burr!"* warning. I saw her attack a gray squirrel with the same ferocity. Her mate sometimes assisted in such sorties, but he was less of a fighter.

I managed an occasional peek into the nest box by waiting until the parents were off gathering meals. I never opened the door for more than a few seconds and did so only in the very early stages of nesting. If you check a nest box when the young are close to fledging, you risk scaring them away before they can fly. Young nestlings, however, are too weak to bolt.

The first time that I saw the five swallow nestlings, who stretched their necks and peeped as I opened the nest box door, I could not help but appoint myself their godfather. For the next ten days I watched their little house carefully. I had a big scare one evening when my landlady got too close to the nest box pole with her weed whacker. When I checked the box at 7 a.m. the next day, I shuddered. The nestlings lay motionless, with their eyes closed. I touched one and it showed no reaction, though it seemed warm.

I was convinced that the noise of the weed whacker had caused the parents to abandon the nest, and that the unbrooded young had died of exposure. I touched another nestling. This one moved slightly. Could they be sleeping?

That's all it was. I checked the box a half hour later and found the adult female sitting on the nest. She flew out a moment after I closed the door, without attacking. That gave me the opportunity to recheck the nest. The heads of the babies sprang up, and they peeped. Later, as I stood by, the female entered the box with food. More peeping, then out she came with a fecal sac that she dropped into the pond. With this task completed she turned on me and aimed straight for my head.

Whether her brood fledged, I can't say. I went to Cape Cod for the long July Fourth weekend, and when I returned the nest was empty. It was intact but compacted, and most of the feathers that had lined it were gone. As I was inspecting it an adult swallow dive-bombed me. Earlier a pair of adults had done the same to a white-tailed deer browsing close to the nest box. One of the swallows had also perched at the hole and peeked inside.

If these were the same swallows that had nested, perhaps they were defending the site out of habit. As for the fledglings, they could have moved to a location that offered better food and cover. I didn't see the adults again. A week later, five or so immature tree swallows flew by while I wandered in the yard. "That's them," I whispered, "the swallows born in the box." I'd like to think so, anyway.

Migrating Tree Swallows gather in huge flocks along the southern New England coast from late August until mid-October. In Connecticut, flocks of 2,000 are considered large, but in October 1994, an estimated 300,000 swallows settled in to roost amid reeds at the mouth of the Connecticut River. I've never seen such numbers. In my experience, the land bird with the most impressive fall migration is the Broad-winged Hawk. On a brisk, sunny afternoon in mid-to-late September, you can gaze with binoculars into billowy clouds and count thousands of Broad-wingeds moving south.

These crow-size raptors with banded tails soar on currents of sun-heated air in groups known as kettles. They usually follow ridges but sometimes migrate along the coast, where they are more likely to pop up over suburban yards. Since they often fly at high altitudes, most people never see them. A single kettle may contain 200 or more individuals that circle as if a great wand had stirred the sky and caught them in a vortex.

Fall has its subtler migration spectacles. Although Blue Jays occur year-round in the eastern United States and in parts of southern Canada, they are migratory. In late September they withdraw from the northern edge of their breeding range and pass through the trees in small bands, a mode of travel that belies their great numbers.

American Kestrels, smallest of North America's falcons, migrate at about the same time as the jays. As they follow the coast, kestrels often hover above marshes and grasslands, waiting to pounce on rodents, small birds, and insects. In fall they can be numerous—I've seen 50 in an hour—but on one late September day at Sherwood Island, I saw only three kestrels the entire morning. A Blue Jay decided to provoke one of them, a male resting on the tip of a sapling beside a salt marsh. It was a showdown between two of our handsomest birds—the ornate Blue Jay, a loud smart aleck, and the dapper American Kestrel, a graceful speed demon.

Although slightly larger than a male kestrel, the Blue Jay has inferior weaponry. Sounding its raspy alarm call, the jay flew at the kestrel, who shrugged off the assault. When the jay persisted, the kestrel retaliated with talons bared. The kestrel drove off the jay, but then a crow flew in and drove off the kestrel. The crow intervened not to protect its fellow corvid—Blue Jays strongly dislike crows, and the feeling, I'm sure, is mutual—but solely because a crow can't resist the temptation to bully a small raptor. If the kestrel's larger cousin, a Peregrine Falcon, had come by and launched an attack, the crow would have been lucky to escape with its life.

After witnessing the brawl I walked on the beach and saw hundreds of Tree Swallows flying west along the edge of Long Island Sound. If I had stayed awhile I probably would have counted a thousand or more, but instead I forged into a rank growth of shrubs and weeds above the beach. The plants were going to seed and had attracted a small convention of sparrows: Savannah, Song, Swamp, White-throated, and Chipping Sparrows.

American Goldfinches in their dull nonbreeding plumage outnumbered any single species of sparrow, and as I waded through the fading foliage they were always the first birds to flush. Keeping just ahead of me, the goldfinches moved in undulating flight, calling as they took off. Among them I found a female Indigo Bunting—a cinnamon brown bird (the name describes the breeding male only)—and a dozen Bobolinks.

Ospreys on their southward journeys flew in widely spaced single file above the marsh, some flapping deeply, others soaring gull-like, with wings bowed. In the muddy channels, the numbers of summering Great and Snowy Egrets had waned; most of those remaining were Greats. One "off" Snowy flying across the marsh caught my eye. It wasn't quite graceful enough, I thought. When I got my binoculars on it, the stout bill, pale blue at the base, and the greenish yellow legs gave away an immature Little Blue Heron.

I came to the edge of an inlet and surprised 26 Double-crested Cormorants, most of them submerged. One by one their snaky heads surfaced, and when all of them were up, the first in line took off, slapping the water with its wingtips and running across the surface before it got airborne. The rest followed, and with labored flight they found refuge in the widest expanse of water.

Two ducks beyond the relocated cormorants were so far away I couldn't identify them. I thought they were Mallard until they dove repeatedly underwater. The very common Mallard is a dabbler, a surface-feeding duck that tips into the water, submerging its front half only. Then I realized I hadn't seen any Mallard all morning. They could have been on the sound or hidden in a tidal creek, but at this time of year, and in this ideal habitat, it was a notable miss. It's easy to forget that the absence of an expected bird can have more significance than the appearance of a rarity.

ON A BIG DAY COUNT I BECOME A HOUND, SNIFFING OUT BIRDS WHILE always on the move. I first heard about a sedentary count from a birder I met at Hammonasset Beach State Park in Madison, Connecticut. He and a few companions had tallied some 60 species birding all day at a single spot. It was a new event called a Big Sit, conjured up by a member of the New Haven Bird Club. At the time I dismissed such enfeebled birding as unworthy of my participation.

By the time I was invited to join other birders at Sherwood Island for the third annual Big Sit, my opinion had changed. During the summer I had taken my reading to a town beach in Westport, passing many afternoons on a sandy crescent across the inlet from Sherwood Island. But I didn't read much. Mostly I watched coastal rhythms: shorebirds following the tide, life-guards twirling their whistles, umbrella fringes and Common Terns flapping in the breeze.

From my bed of sand on those late summer days, I saw things I had missed in miles of walking. A Short-billed Dowitcher shot along the inlet—I heard its subdued triple toot—the only dowitcher I saw all season. Least Sandpipers landed at my bare feet. Fifty Semipalmated Plover settled beside the Sherwood Island jetty and became invisible among the rocks. Children exploring the tide pools didn't notice the plover, or the probing Ruddy Turnstone, or the teetering Spotted Sandpiper. The carousel of life keeps turning, in time showing sides you might never see while moving with it. You need not always go to the birds. If you're patient nature's ultimate travelers will come to you—the inspiration for the Big Sit.

The Big Sit is like a hawk-watch because you stay in one place: a strategically located 17-foot-diameter circle. It's like a Big Day because you count all species, not only hawks. Members of your team are supposed to stay in the circle from dawn to dusk on the second Sunday in October, and you compete with other teams for the highest species total. You can leave the circle to get a closer look at a bird you're unable to identify, but you can't count other birds while outside the circle.

Scouting Sherwood Island the day before the event, I couldn't imagine approaching the 70 species found a year earlier by big-sitters at Milford Point, a Connecticut birding hot spot at the mouth of the Housatonic River. In three hours I had logged only 53 species, and that was while moving through the park in my usual doglike way.

The next morning I arrived before my two teammates and picked our spot: the picnic area behind West Beach. I had seen a Sharp-shinned Hawk and a kestrel there the previous day, and we'd have a view of most of Sherwood Island's habitats: Long Island Sound and the beach in front, the marsh and the Sherwood Mill Pond in back, woods on the left, and dry brush on the right. It was also a very pleasant place to be, this grassy carpet dotted with oak saplings and picnic tables.

A west wind blew stiff and steady all morning, so I never really warmed up. Under low, swiftly moving clouds, the choppy sound was slate gray, a good background for spotting waterfowl, but all we had were Mallard and Black Ducks, plus the usual gulls. The land birds at times swirled around us, but generally they trickled through, crossing east to west over the open area where we stood. In the saplings Yellow-rumped Warblers and a few Palm Warblers were our constant companions, and Tufted Titmice streamed by. Most of the park's common birds passed our checkpoint—if we didn't see them, we heard their distinctive calls.

Unusual species were an American Oystercatcher flying way out above the sound, the fall's first Red-throated Loon, and a formation of 40 Snow Geese against the clouds. A Peregrine Falcon flew directly over us at 7:30 a.m.—we had expected one but not so quickly.

We waited hours for several common birds—Blue Jay, Northern Flicker, and Fish Crow—but missed the Red-winged Blackbird and American Robin. We were lucky to get an Eastern Meadowlark and a Common Snipe, which usually stay on the east side of the park. Our only sparrows were Songs and Savannahs. More sparrows undoubtedly skulked in the weeds about 200 yards to our right, but we decided it would be cheating to send someone over to flush them into view.

Our scopes pulled in a lone Greater Yellowlegs on the mill pond, and we had fair success with raptors: 20 Ospreys; 5 Northern Harriers; 10 Sharp-shinned, 3 Cooper's, and 2 Red-tailed Hawks; 5 kestrels; and the Peregrine. Two of the harriers were flying west just above the sound, migrating over open water, I suppose, to avoid harassment by crows. A Cooper's Hawk forced down a couple of Black Ducks crossing the marsh, but then passed over them—a practice attack maneuver. To see what other birds were possible that day, we took a midmorning foray into the rest of the park and found nine more birds, common species that had evaded our circle's radar. Of course, we could not include them in our official total.

We stopped after six hours, at 12:30, with 55 species seen or heard from our beachside roost, two more than I had counted the day before on my customary rounds. Perhaps we could have broken 60 if we stayed all day, but we had no hope of surpassing Milford Point's 70 species, the Connecticut record at the time. Although we fell short of the Big Sit champs, I never would have guessed that we could stay put and see 55 species at Sherwood

Island in mid-October. I expected 30, 40 birds at most, but then again, I am a novice at sitting still outdoors. Rarely do I come to a dead halt for an hour or more. I pause to rest or admire a view, but in a minute I'm back on my feet.

I like to walk when I go birding, but this is only one way to experience infinitely dynamic nature. When I meet a fisherman on one of my waterside rambles, he may mention birds I haven't seen. He hardly moves and sees a different world—nature's law of relativity. In the wild you can journey without using your feet.

With one of my Big Sit teammates, I did the Christmas Bird Count at Sherwood Island for a number of years. The CBC is a venerable count, begun on Christmas Day in 1900 by ornithologist Frank M. Chapman in reaction to the Christmas Side Hunt, a competition in which hunters chose sides. The side that shot the most birds won.

The first CBC had 27 participants, most of whom lived in the Northeast. They recorded 90 species and 18,500 individual birds. Today more than 50,000 participants cover sites in North America, the Pacific Islands, and Latin America. In 2002 the CBC recorded more than 70 million individual birds and, in North America and Hawaii, more than 650 species. The CBC database, which is maintained by the National Audubon Society, has grown into one of the most important tools for tracking changes in bird populations of the Western Hemisphere.

I helped cover Sherwood Island and Wakeman's Farm for the CBC from 1986 to 1996, studiously following the instructions provided by the birder who compiled the count results for Westport: "Be in the field at sunrise ... spend time owling ... stake out unusual birds ... pursue the commoner birds more aggressively." On my first CBC I went to Sherwood Island at 4:30 a.m.—in the rain, no less—with hopes of spotting an owl returning to its daytime roost. In subsequent counts I tried the more effective owling technique of combing evergreen stands during the day. But in all those years I never found an owl on the CBC.

Aside from a low count of 37 species and a high count of 58, I can't remember much of my CBC days at Sherwood Island. That's the trouble with organized counts, and the reason I stopped doing this one. It had become too routine and mathematical. All I had at the end of an exhausting day of birding was a sheetful of numbers. I needed a break from birding's tradition of counting. I wanted to go deeper.

CHAPTER 11

THE BARRED OWL

I rejoice that there are owls.
HENRY DAVID THOREAU

REPORTS ONE WINTER OF OWLS APPEARING IN NUMBERS ACROSS MUCH of the Northeast—primarily saw-whets but also Long-eareds and even a few Great Grays—inspired me to find an owl I could call my own. Owls usually roost by day under the protective cover of evergreens, so one frigid morning I went to Sherwood Island State Park and inspected each qualifying tree.

I trudged from one tree to another in ankle-deep snow, checking trunks and lower branches for "whitewash"—owl scat. At the base of each tree I looked for owl pellets—regurgitated fur and bones from the small mammals owls eat. Owls also eat birds, and large owls prey on smaller owls.

In three hours I had found a little whitewash, no pellets, and no owls. Crisscrossing the park's woods, I hadn't flushed a thing. Under one spruce I found the remains of a bird, possibly a screech-owl that had fallen victim to a larger predator, and near a big cedar I picked up an immature Red-tailed Hawk, frozen solid. With no visible wounds, the inexperienced Red-tailed may have died of starvation, cut off from its rodent prey by deep snow.

After a three-day thaw, I returned to see what the receding snow would reveal. Under the setting sun, a hundred Canada geese grazed a large lawn bordered by a row of giant white pines. I had overlooked these pines during my systematic owl check. They stand in the open and do not offer the cover I would want if I were an owl, but in today's gathering gloom they beckoned, looking ominous enough to be a nocturnal bird's retreat.

Murmuring their objections, the geese cleared away as I approached. At the fifth pine in from the park road, I struck gold. Only a birder could get a thrill from a clump of fur and bones the size of a fat thumb. A birder I know had recently seen a Great Horned Owl in the park—a pellet this big had to come from that bird. Other pellets surrounded the tree, some broken apart by recent rain.

Looking up, I didn't see a roosting owl, but it was already late enough for a Great Horned to have embarked on its nightly hunt. I glanced at the geese. They ambled across the grass, here and there pulling up shoots. The Canada Goose's large size does not guarantee it immunity from the Great Horned Owl, whose hunting prowess is legendary. With their backs to the pine, the geese made tempting targets.

There was time enough before dark to check a dense stand of spruces, which one winter harbored a saw-whet owl. Below one tree, the ground now clear of snow, I found whitewash, small bones, and a feather. The bones probably came from old pellets— over time, snow and rain wash away the fur and scatter the bones—but the whitewash and the feather were fresh.

The next morning at the white pine, I pointed out the large owl pellet to another birder. He nodded solemnly. We noticed more owl clues under a different pine, and when we reached the bone-littered spruce, our internal owl Geiger counters were at full crackle. Any trees we checked, however, were deserted.

Noisy crows soon brought us to a halt. We listened carefully, because there are no better owl finders than crows. At night large owls prey on crows; crows seek revenge by mobbing owls that trespass into day.

Crows that catch a Great Horned Owl abroad by day send up an alarm capable of summoning hundreds more crows, each intent on making the owl's life miserable. Crows will chase and scold and dive-bomb a Great Horned Owl, their most hated enemy, until it is driven out of the neighborhood or back to its lair. Owls at their roosts, however, are not spared. If crows find a sleeping owl, they will return to its bedroom door throughout the day to give it a verbal drubbing.

In the trees ahead of us, the cawing of the crows was not venomous enough for them to have cornered a Great Horned Owl. They were agitated but not infuriated—perhaps 20 were complaining from the treetops about something lower down, which we couldn't see. My guess was that they were responding to a lesser threat: a Red-tailed Hawk. We used the crows to triangulate on the target, pausing at the last moment behind a 15-foot spruce. If the crows hadn't fooled us, we'd find what we were looking for on the other side of this tree.

It wasn't a Red-tailed that we saw when we came around the spruce. It was an owl but not a Great Horned. Perched in a deciduous tree, surrounded by crows, this was a Barred Owl, a bird neither of us had ever seen in the park. It leaned forward and stared with deep brown eyes as we voiced our amazement. Then it shifted position and dropped off the tree, flying low and away from us, pursued by the tormenting crows.

At my inland haunts—in forests, along hemlock-lined streams, in the wooded swamp—I expect Barred Owl encounters, but on the coast this owl is rare. In March its forest chant begins echoing through the cavernous night—eight rhythmic hoots, the last a descending *hoo-aw*. ("The *aw* at the close is characteristic," said Peterson.) A large owl, the Barred is nearly as long as a Great Horned but is much lighter and takes smaller prey.

Quintessential creature of the night, the Barred Owl has a somber visage, mud brown puffy feathers spotted with white, a large round head and no apparent neck, a pale breast with blurry streaks, and a barred ruff (which gives the bird its name). The combined effect of these characteristics is a definite ghoulishness; the owl's retiring habits, noiseless flight, and macabre vocalizations only add to its character. In the depths of the moon-drenched swamp, the Barred Owl is where it is meant to be.

When this Barred Owl flew off, we let it go. The crows were causing the bird enough anxiety, and we'd had a long look. We had studied the owl for a good five seconds.

Although essentially nonmigratory, the Barred Owl may leave its forested territory in winter if prey becomes scarce. Its search for small mammals and, to a lesser extent, birds may even bring it to city parks, where it can feast on mice, squirrels, and House Sparrows.

One nomadic owl spent a few December days around the Winkler homestead in Westport. A very tame individual, it remained perched on a fence post while my sister and I stood watching it in the floodlit backyard. Now and then it flew like a giant moth and plunged feet first into leaves blown up against the fence, going for mice or shrews. It always came up empty but was unfazed, and as it returned to the perch its buoyant flight suggested that it enjoyed this hit-or-miss game. It conveyed none of the ferocity of the goshawk, no sense that its survival hung in the balance.

This mellow nature led ornithologist Arthur Cleveland Bent to describe the Barred Owl as "a very gentle bird for a raptor." His classic *Life Histories of North American Birds* quotes a similar opinion from owl researcher Paul L. Errington: "The Barred Owl seems endowed with about as mild a personality as a raptor could have and yet maintain a predaceous existence." Bent tells of three attacks on humans, but these owls were defensive parents pushed to the extreme by a collector or researcher climbing their nest tree. Bent's own nest studies in southeastern Massachusetts were relatively peaceful. "I have never had one even threaten to attack me," he wrote, "even when I was handling the young."

The Barred Owls I've come to know live in the Upper Paugusset State Forest. At times they snap their bills and stare angrily when I walk near their nest, but usually they don't object. They have good habitat here, along the west bank of the Housatonic River. Streams cross the forested slopes, and there are many old-growth trees. Barred Owls usually nest in cavities of large trees or in hollows of broken trunks; sometimes they use old hawk nests. They also appropriate nests of crows and squirrels.

If Fairfield County has a better place for Barred Owls than the Upper Paugusset, I haven't found it. Indeed, I've heard more hooting in my home woods than I have on trips to much wilder parts of New England. I suppose I encounter a Barred Owl on one of every three or four walks. *Strix varia* and I have much in common: We appreciate our little corner of the Earth, cherish big trees, love the night, and can be very vocal.

When I describe the owl to people who are unfamiliar with it, I spell "barred" to prevent confusion with "bard," but we might as well use the second word, because of all North American owls this one has the most impressive vocal repertoire. Since my walks generally begin late in the day, they often end after dark, especially in winter. Therefore, I've had ample exposure to Barred Owl language.

Officially, the Upper Paugusset and other preserves in my area "close" at dusk. I do not abide by this curfew. As the photographer Brassai noted, "Night birds and nocturnal animals bring a forest to life when its daytime fauna fall silent and go to ground." The authorities place no restrictions on my movements in the peopled world. Why should I let them do so in the woods and cut me off from owls and other night life?

Their arbitrary decree stems, I think, from the deeply ingrained human fear of the dark. But I make a moot point. The curfew doesn't affect me because no one enforces it. There's no need to. Who would be crazy enough to walk in a forest at night?

You can actually feel quite at home there once you get acclimated. You must learn to rely on hearing over vision and to recognize sounds that we diurnal animals don't often hear—not only of owls but also of frogs, toads, insects, and mammals. A deer's humanlike footsteps and startling snort soon grow familiar. You learn to take in stride a coyote crashing through the undergrowth, a surprised raccoon escaping up a tree while growling like a bear. You must also get used to the tricks of your flashlight. In its beam shadows take on monstrous proportions. A sapling looms up and comes to life at your approach, reaching for you with ghostly black limbs.

With experience the starlit forest becomes nature's funhouse, but if you would rather not be a creature of the night, you can still glimpse Barred Owls. You might catch one sunning in a roadside tree after a rainstorm, its half-shut eyes giving the impression of sleepiness. The owl is probably wide awake. It lets its eyelids droop to blend with the surroundings and may shut them further if you walk closer, on the chance that it has escaped notice. Only a slit of each eye may be visible, but get too close and the owl will promptly drop the disguise and fly in the opposite direction, with no sound but a vibrating branch to mark its departure.

The Barred Owl may vocalize at any time, but it gives the best performances after sundown. Its hooting, while not musical, is one of the great animal sounds, rivaling the domestic cat's purr and the American toad's trill. The typical series of eight hoots, given in two groups of four, has been described as "reverberant" (Edward Howe Forbush); "strongly accented, loud, wild, and strenuous" (Arthur Cleveland Bent); "emphatic" (Roger Tory Peterson); and "clear-voiced, expressive" (David Allen Sibley). A favorite translation of the Barred Owl's hooting—*who cooks for you, who cooks for you-all*—captures its rhythm but none of its raw character.

It is spirited hooting, less deep and sinister than that of the Great Horned Owl. We more often hear the Great Horned Owl on movie soundtracks because its hooting works better as a background sound—a mood enhancer that doesn't get in the way. The Barred Owl's clearer, more insistent hooting is a fore-ground sound. It would detract from the main action.

Sometimes the Barred Owl lets out a single, smooth *hoo* that drops in pitch; at other times it gives only the final throaty *hoo-aw* of the eight-hoot series. A vocalization known as the ascending hoot consists of six to nine short hoots that rise slightly in pitch and increase in speed as they approach the closing *hoo*-aw. Pairs engage in duets, particularly in early spring. The male, though smaller, has the deeper voice. His eight hoots bring an immediate response from the female, who echoes the call. Back and forth they go, occasionally whipping themselves into such a frenzy that their calls overlap. I'm always tempted to chime in but hold my tongue. Romancing owls have a right to privacy.

I can do a passable rendition of the Barred Owl's call, at least by human standards. I proved this at the Saugatuck Reservoir. I was trying to call up Barred Owls and instead called up two boys. I was within earshot of a road and they were passing on bicycles. When they heard my hoots they stopped and hooted back. I'm sure they didn't see me.

I could never fool an owl so completely. Still, I'm much better than the turkey hunter I heard this spring. He was trying a favorite hunter's trick: male turkeys sometimes gobble in response to an owl's hoots, so hunters mimic owls to get turkeys to betray their whereabouts. I shook my head at the hunter's slurred, whiny hoots. I had just seen a Barred Owl. The hunter's embarrassing performance made me want to go back and apologize.

According to Bent, the owl's hooting "is easily imitated, and anyone who can do it well should have no difficulty calling up any Barred Owls within hearing." No human voice, however, can duplicate the wildness of the hooting—its owlish quality. I rarely do the call because it disturbs the owls (it's even worse to play an owl recording, which represents a more serious territorial threat). If I get a response, it happens less frequently than Bent suggests.

The longer I kept up a conversation with one owl, the more it distorted its voice, until finally it seemed to be laughing at my efforts. It might have been the same owl that accosted me in the dead of a winter night with screams that sounded human. At first I was convinced a lunatic had climbed a tree. The screams degenerated into wolflike howling. I was about to run when a hoot and several *aws* issued from the same direction. I hooted back but got no answer. Maybe the owl was showing off for a silent companion. I'm inclined to believe it was trying to frighten me from the woods.

The eeriest Barred Owl sound comes from the young. Well-developed nestlings and juveniles up to four months old solicit food from their parents with a rasping whistle, or a hiss, that slides up the scale and concludes with a slight pop. This food-begging call does not translate well—a correspondent of Bent's wrote it as *shooeet;* Sibley's transcription is an unpronounceable *kssssshhip.* The call lasts no more than two seconds and may be given repeatedly, between pauses of 15 to 30 seconds. Although attributed to the young, it also seems to come from at least one of the doting parents (probably the mother), who tend their brood into late summer and perhaps beyond.

I've heard the call as early as the first week of May and as late as mid-August. Although I think of it as one of the characteristic summer bird sounds, popular ornithological literature pays it scant attention. Audubon may have been the first to note its unnerving quality. "To a person lost in a swamp," he wrote, "it is, indeed, extremely dismal." Bent gives it more detailed treatment through secondhand reports—despite his extensive studies of nesting Barred Owls, he never heard the call himself. Sibley's is the only field guide I know of that describes the call; my book on North American owls gives it nothing more than a brief mention. I've yet to hear a good recording.

Partly because of this dearth of information, it took me five years to connect the call with the Barred Owl. Until I finally witnessed juveniles producing it, I thought it came from another, smaller owl. My guess was the saw-whet. What threw me off was the great difference between the almost reptilian hiss and the booming vocalizations typical of the Barred Owl.

Before I learned the source of this awful sound, it had spooked me more than once. Its most disconcerting aspect: It is nearly impossible to pinpoint. I have stood in the blackened forest as it seemed to come from all directions. Three owls can sound like six because they move about on silent wings and call from successive perches. One foggy night at the reservoir, a Barred Owl family came so close I thought I would feel their windy breath. They seemed conscious of the call's chilling effect. A food-begging call? In this case it clearly signified aggression.

Juveniles are capable of other vocalizations. At the Upper Paugusset, in broad daylight, I surprised two that were honing their flying skills while being mobbed by small birds. They were clumsy, kittenish versions of adult owls, more buff in color overall, with shorter tails and extensive white flecking on their upperparts. One flew to a branch a safe distance away from me, spun around, lowered its wings, and held them in bowed fashion. Although designed to intimidate, the pose struck me as comical, since the owl had trouble keeping its balance. Next it produced a soft hoot, which I couldn't resist imitating. With that the owl gave me a wounded stare that made me instantly regret my insolence.

There's one Barred Owl vocalization I could never hope to imitate. The apotheosis of North American owl sounds, it's our equivalent of the kookaburra's laugh. Adults sometimes launch into this mode of communication, known as caterwauling. I have been privileged to hear it several times, usually at night. Forbush, who once watched courting Barred Owls in the light of his wilderness campfire, described their caterwauling as "the most weird and uncouth sounds imaginable....Sounds resembling maniacal laughter and others like mere chuckles were interspersed here and there between loud *wha whas* and *hoo-hoó-aws.*"

The maniacal laughs remind me of the *wah-wahs* of a trumpet player using a mute. During these raucous exchanges the owls seem to have quite a good time. An audience does not cramp their style—they have entertained me for eight minutes as I stood close by. I last heard caterwauling in the winter of 2003. After January's extreme cold, February had been pelting New England with snow. I was near the end of a demoralizing snowshoe trek along the Upper Paugusset logging road. Because I'd forgotten my gaiters, slush covered my lower legs and filled my boots. In the 15°F cold, my fingers had gone numb. Fatigue had me walking sloppily, inefficiently. I'd been trying for weeks to go the distance with winter, but now winter was winning.

The one consolation was the moon. It was only half full, but aided by the snow it lit up the woods. I did the whole walk without turning on the flashlight, though I couldn't make out the Barred Owl that now seemed to be shooing me toward the car. No more than a hundred feet away, he gave the classic eight hoots. Farther off, a female's higher pitched hooting answered. The male then broke into a wild improvisation, his *wah-wahs* and cackles stealing the spotlight from winter's stage. The female instantly picked up on his riff, playing bass to his horn. He, in turn, moved in her direction.

It seemed a ritual greeting that spoke of unbridled joy. I was amazed that owls could laugh and hoot in the face of this frigid, snowy night, another in a long line of such nights. They didn't know where their next meal was coming from. They themselves could be hunted by the Great Horned Owl and the goshawk. Yet their faith in nature's providence was unshaken.

They were glad to be alive, and lustily—defiantly—they announced it to the whole world. Forget what you might have heard about owls as portenders of doom. Owls are optimists. Properly interpreted, their language has the power to light dark nights and dark souls.

CHAPTER 12

OTHER LIVES

OF HIS FRONTIER EXPLORATIONS FOR *THE BIRDS OF AMERICA,* JOHN JAMES Audubon wrote, "I never was troubled in the woods by any animal larger than ticks and mosquitoes." Reports from Asia of tigers carrying off people led Henry David Thoreau to state, "The traveller can lie down in the woods at night almost anywhere in North America without fear of wild beasts." Wild beasts were the furthest thing from my mind one summer day as I pulled into the parking lot of a Fairfield County nature preserve. Nearby, another suburb dweller sat in a gleaming white air-conditioned jeep, talking on the phone.

I began my walk and within minutes deer flies buzzed threateningly around my ears, and two mosquitoes lodged in my left eye. As I waited for the burning to subside, I quickened my pace and lowered my head to avoid another kamikaze attack. It was a warm and humid afternoon, and though it hadn't rained significantly for weeks, the trail was damp and any bare mud had a slippery green film. A few bird songs penetrated the thick air, but with only one good eye and with insect piranhas waiting for me to pause, I did not look for the undaunted singers. It had become a walk for exercise, not nature study, and I was disposed to get it over with.

Halfway along my 90-minute route, I noticed the shed scales of a snake on a rocky ledge. At this same spot I once had happened upon a black rat snake, six feet long and double the thickness of a garden hose. I scanned the ledge for this shy constrictor but instead found, nestled in a shallow fissure, a 2.5-foot copperhead. In an instant I forgot the heat, the stickiness, the birds, and the bloodthirsty bugs.

The copperhead is one of the most widespread venomous snakes in the United States. There are five subspecies—*Agkistrodon contortrix mokasen,* the northern copperhead, occurs in Connecticut. It belongs to a family of snakes that has the most highly evolved venom-delivery system. Until a copperhead strikes, its hollow fangs stay folded along its upper jaw. When it lunges toward a victim, the fangs spring forward, poised to inject venom. The venom is dangerous but rarely life threatening to healthy adult humans. A person bitten by a copperhead may not even be treated with antivenin, which carries risks of its own.

(Snakebite fatalities are rare in the United States—each year, venomous snakes bite about 8,000 Americans, resulting in about a dozen deaths. In at least a quarter of these bites, the snakes fail to inject venom. Of course, anyone who doesn't keep a safe distance from a venomous snake plays a very foolish game. Even dead snakes have been known to bite reflexively.)

Although the copperhead is near the northern limit of its range in Connecticut, the nature preserves in which I walk provide it plenty of good habitat: wooded streamside slopes with rock outcroppings, where the copperhead preys on small rodents, young birds, frogs, and insects. On the hottest days copperheads may hunt at night, retiring by day to a shady spot, possibly the same one that attracts an overheated hiker. In winter they hibernate or den up, often choosing rock recesses, which they may share with other snake species.

Most people who go to the woods never see a copperhead, because the snake either remains motionless in its red-and-brown camouflage or slithers away. It may lack external ears, but a copperhead can still hear a person's approach. Its body transmits the vibrations of human footsteps through its jawbone to the columella, a bone that, in turn, conducts these low, ground-borne frequencies to the snake's inner ear.

This was not my first copperhead encounter. Some years ago, on another trail, I narrowly missed stepping on one. Before the snake escaped, I moved behind it and dangled a very long stick above its head, trying to get it to strike. Although normally nonaggressive, the copperhead will strike vigorously if provoked. An alarmed copperhead may vibrate its tail, which doesn't have a rattle but may produce a rattling sound as it hits surrounding vegetation.

Looking back, I realize my baiting of that copperhead was foolish and cruel, but I was curious. The snake outsmarted me: though coiled up like a spring, following the motion of the stick with its head, it refused to strike. Why waste precious venom on an inanimate object?

The haunts of this latest copperhead were similar to those of the first: an eastern slope on a rocky hill, surrounded by mountain laurel thickets and mixed woods, with a stream nearby. Loosely coiled in the cleft of a tranquil hillside, resting quietly in the hazy light of a summer afternoon, it presented no overt threat.

Yet something about the copperhead said, don't crowd me. Maybe it was the bold patterning of the skin, or the thickness of the body, or the broad skull, or the way the snake just lay there, exuding quiet confidence in its ability to repel a much larger animal.

With a healthy buffer zone between us, I sat on the sloping ledge and studied the copper-colored upturned head, the eye with its pupil narrowed into a vertical slit, and the brown hourglass-shape crossbands along the pale brick-red body. The crossbands are narrow on the back, wide on the sides. Usually there are conspicuous brown dots between some of the crossbands. This snake's appearance was typical, but the color and pattern of northern copperheads can vary.

Through my binoculars I saw a small hole, or pit, between the eye and nostril—the heat-sensing organ, used to locate warm-blooded prey, that identifies the copperhead as a pit viper. The rarer and more dangerous timber rattlesnake, the only other venomous snake of the Northeast, belongs to the same subfamily, as do cottonmouths—venomous snakes of southern swamps, among other habitats. Of some 20 venomous snakes in the United States, all but the coral snakes are pit vipers.

So intently was I focused on this copperhead that ten minutes must have elapsed before I noticed a second shed snakeskin, and then a third, farther down the ledge. When I felt satisfied that the motionless copperhead had no inclination to approach, I stretched out my legs, leaned back on my elbows, and let my eyes wander. My gaze fell on an alarming sight. It was another copperhead, but this one was huge, surely one for the record books. It appeared to be eight feet long, and it rested in a crevice a yard from my heels.

I folded my legs and slid away. I knew that copperheads rarely exceed three feet, so how could this monster exist?

Now that I was out of striking range, I looked more carefully and counted three heads. It wasn't the Hydra; it was three average-size copperheads curled up together, taking their siesta. Spilled into the crevice, they looked like disembodied intestines. One was wedged between the rock and the base of a sapling, the kink in its body apparently having no ill effect on the circulation. The snakes never moved, never even tasted the air with their forked tongues.

Disturbed that I had been reclining unsuspectingly with vipers, I became snake paranoid. The copperhead is gregarious; I had found four on this ledge, but maybe there were more. I checked and rechecked the rocky ledge, scrutinizing every crack and depression. On the return trail I tread lightly and kept checking against the reds and browns of the forest floor, the well-camouflaged copperhead could be anywhere.

I found myself stopping at every suspicious rock, every pile of decaying wood, every bed of rust-colored leaves, the base of every bush. If I continued this way, I'd never make it out of the woods, and stepping so stealthily probably increased my risk of surprising a copperhead. My only choice was to walk normally and trust that the thuds of my boots would warn other snakes to withdraw. My feet carried me safely to the nature preserve's trailhead, as they always had.

On another summer walk through the woods, I was surprised at how late the birds sang. I had to resort to my flashlight before the lazy voice of the wood-pewee faded away, and a duel between Wood Thrushes—supreme songsters of the forest—lasted until 9 p.m. Making my way through a hemlock grove, the inkiest part of the trail, I heard a squeaking, chattering sound. I pointed my light in its direction and caught a two-second glimpse of a flying squirrel before it dashed from a branch to the other side of a massive tree trunk.

Although I had only a fleeting look, the image of the flying squirrel in my spotlight stayed riveted in my mind. The squirrel's "wings"—flaps of skin between the front and hind legs—have a black border, and the fur appears silky, but what struck me most were the eyes: large black disks that gather enough light for the squirrel to glide safely through starlit woods. I recall the sound of its claws biting into the hemlock bark as it escaped my own eyes, so ineffective in darkness. Surely owls and foxes know the flying squirrel well. Perhaps even our dogs and cats, who can see in the dark, have more than a passing acquaintance with it. It is the rare human, however, who has met a flying squirrel face to face in the wild. Our night blindness and our aversion to gloomy forests make such encounters rather difficult.

At home I read what little I could find on this nocturnal phantom and learned that flying squirrels are common, perhaps the commonest squirrels in southern New England, yet in all my previous walks I had never seen one. Empty hickory nuts with a smooth-edged circular opening at one end indicate their presence, but they are easier to detect by their squeaks. Like red and gray squirrels, they sometimes come out to scold passersby. Cloaked in darkness, they chatter softly and whistle on a very high pitch. Some of their calls could be confused with those of birds. Their twitter is like a Dark-eyed Junco's and, like a Tufted Titmouse, they produce a thin, rising squeak. If you hear these sounds coming from the trees at night, chances are it's a flying squirrel.

Two species of flying squirrels, southern and northern, occur in the United States. They are our only strictly nocturnal squirrels; in the Northeast their ranges overlap. The one I had found was probably the smaller southern flying squirrel. About the size of an eastern chipmunk, it has a warm brown back and a whitish belly.

The next evening I returned to the woods to get better acquainted with this elusive tree hugger. I sat on a rock near the massive hemlock and gazed at the darkening canopy. Would I see the squirrel launch from a treetop and glide 200 feet to the trunk of another tree, using its outstretched membrane of loose skin to steer around obstacles, veering up at the last moment to soften its landing? The wood-pewee and Wood Thrushes sang on schedule, and 20 minutes after sunset came the same squeaks that had led me to the squirrel the night before.

I followed the sounds deep into the hemlock grove and stabbed at the darkness with my flashlight. I drew the beam up tree trunks and across limbs, but tonight the squirrel refused to reveal itself. Through rustling leaves, the lights of a house became visible, and I realized that a strange blue glow in the yard was a device for electrocuting insects. When a dog barked, I felt discovered and started on the mile-long trail back to the car. If flying squirrels were indeed common, I should encounter others.

As night advanced, my ears became sensitized to the degree that my eyes weakened. The Barred Owl hooting on the far side of the reservoir must have been more than a mile away, but I heard it plainly. A siren sent a family of coyotes into a paroxysm of howls that, distorted by distance, sounded like a pack of laughing girls. Distant rumblings were probably summer fireworks, rather than an approaching storm, and though I was far beyond the bug zapper I heard an occasional spatter as it claimed another victim.

My books were not mistaken about the flying squirrel's abundance. From the trees that night I heard five squeaks identical to the ones made by the squirrel I had seen. They were separated by intervals of walking, so I believe they came from different individuals. I found nuts neatly opened in the manner of the flying squirrel, and old stumps and tree cavities that seemed likely squirrel homes, but the little gliders kept hidden.

I'm sure they saw me, stumbling over rocks and roots, waving my flashlight, trying to attract them with ludicrous imitations of their squeaks. In their world, I am a helpless and puzzling escapee from the land of electric light. In mine, they are aliens, or so I like to pretend. The first mile of a November walk along the west bank of the Housatonic gave no hint that, in a sense, I would capture one.

Two Great Horned Owls, a mated pair, were hooting from the other side of the river. As their voices boomed into the surrounding hills, a yellow moon pushed up through a cloud and spread its reflection over the water. It would be a dark two miles through the Upper Paugusset State Forest back to my car. I crossed the boulder-strewn brook where two evenings before I had flushed a Barred Owl and passed the old double-trunked white oak, ghostly in the moonlight.

Soon after turning onto the logging road, I suspected that something was watching me. Through the interference of leaves crackling underfoot, I heard tiny claws biting into wood. I drew my flashlight and pointed it in the direction of the sound. The beam landed squarely on a flying squirrel.

Fifteen feet up, the squirrel was clinging to a tree trunk, head toward the ground. Apparently stunned by my light, it froze for almost 30 seconds, an exceptionally long period for a member of such a hyperkinetic family. I hoped it would climb higher and leap spread-eagled from the tree, drawing its skin flaps taut and becoming, before my eyes, a flattened parachute of fur with a bushy tail.

From its outspread toes to its blunt-pointed ears, the squirrel hadn't twitched a muscle. It seemed like a wooden carving until I focused on its big eyes, which were charged with life. Trying to catch their reddish orange shine in my light, I shuffled my feet in the leaves. The squirrel snapped out of its trance and, with a twitter, scrambled to the opposite side of the trunk. I tried to keep up with it but the steep shoulder of the logging road slowed me down, and when I got around the tree I couldn't find it. Either it had entered a cavity midway up the trunk, or it had launched itself to another tree.

The flying squirrel's predators share its proclivity for darkness. Owls of all sorts are the primary threat. Even the diminutive saw-whet owl, hardly bigger than a robin, has been known to swallow a flying squirrel whole.

Beset by ravenous enemies, flying squirrels somehow thrive. They are not confined to the forest. I have heard them along country roads and have glimpsed them sailing by the wooded edge of a floodlit suburban yard, where they might be mistaken for little UFOs. They make nocturnal appearances at bird feeders that are situated close enough to woods. Occasionally they get into attics; in the wild they usually nest in woodpecker holes. They're highly gregarious in winter, when 20 might den in the same tree.

Once I met a hunter who had stumbled onto one of their dormitories. While taking aim at something, he braced himself against a rotting tree that began to topple. Several flying squirrels bailed out of the top and glided over his head. "It was scary," he said, confirming that, even in daylight, the flying squirrel is a virtual creature from another planet.

As I sat at my desk on a sunny morning, my life was interrupted by a more familiar tree dweller. My screenful of words vanished, and the digital clock on my answering machine clicked off. The electric hum always in the background of human existence—refrigerator motor, furnace, computer fan—sighed away. The room fell silent at 9:50 a.m., but my internal power plant kicked in with a flash of exasperation. I had not saved what I was working on.

What could possibly have gone wrong on this warm and windless day? The electric company had received no other reports from my street but said they would send someone out. I made other calls and an hour later, with an excuse not to work, left for the bookstore. Just outside the driveway, a yellow electric company truck with flashing lights idled beside a utility pole. I asked the driver the cause of the power failure.

"Squirrel on the transformer," he said, as he filled out a form on his clipboard.

"Was it killed?" I asked.

"Yes."

"Electrocuted?"

He nodded and motioned to the base of the pole.

"It's over there."

I left the car running and got out to look. Eyes half closed, the unlucky acrobat lay on its side next to the pole—a female gray squirrel who chose the wrong tree. Under her chin, possibly at the point of contact, the fur was burned completely away, exposing a patch of bare white skin about an inch and a half in diameter. Black-singed fur bordered this area and extended down the right side. The white underside fur, scorched brown or sheared almost to the skin, seemed the work of a mad electrified barber.

The partly consumed gray fur on the sides and legs resembled steel wool. A burn line followed the left hind leg almost to the toes. The head, back, and tail seemed relatively unaffected. The electric company man got out of the truck and came over.

"Burned through," he said. "It must have come along, touched the hot wire that leads from the transformer to the overhead wire, and then touched the grounded transformer. That's 13,000 volts."

He said it happens often, and that sometimes an animal will get into a substation and knock out a whole town. "I'll turn the power on in ten minutes," he said. "Just have to flick a switch at the end of the street."

Our brief conversation next to running vehicles on the otherwise deserted street was the only service for this fallen denizen of the trees. I wondered about her history and whether others would mourn her. We could have been neighbors for years. Maybe I had seen her bounding through the yard. I might have watched her spiraling around a tree trunk at play with another squirrel or heard her barking at the neighborhood cats. The sound of her teeth grinding the hickory nut might have caught my attention on the way to the mailbox.

That morning outside my window, I had watched three squirrels as they feverishly dug up nuts and scampered back into the woods. I wondered whether she had been among them, whether her home was that clump of leaves and sticks in a bare tree near the utility pole. She may have been returning to her nest to feed her young, who, if they survived without her, would probably never learn her fate.

On this beautiful day, having made it through winter, she must have rejoiced at the promise of spring as she hastened to fulfill maternal duties. She could have taken this route in safety a hundred times before, then chanced one day to place herself in the deadly position. Perhaps an amorous male had pursued her or some ground dweller had alarmed her into climbing to where she thought she would be safe. As she traveled the live tightwire, perhaps she placed one leg here before letting go there and thus became a victim of her own caution. A buzzing, burning flash gripped her, drew the life from her, flung her away.

The one connection with the squirrel I was certain about was the moment of her death, marked by the shutdown of my computer. Her final pulse of life brought human doings on this quiet street to a temporary halt—her immolation a wild creature's ultimate statement on technology. Standing over her I realized how rarely we pause, in our self-absorbed, technology-driven lives, to acknowledge the rightful place of so ordinary a creature as a gray squirrel. Furry lives end every day in the suburban jungle, but I did not want this one to be forgotten at the flick of a switch. I picked up the squirrel by her bushy tail and moved her to a grassy resting place farther away from the road.

ON A BRILLIANT JULY MORNING I STAND BAREFOOT AND SHIRTLESS ON THE lawn of the Newtown house. I watch my cat, Mimi, step gingerly through the dewy grass toward the pond. The air is so cool that when the sun hits my skin I sense heat but no burning. The cool air and hot sun put me in a summer languor. I pay no attention to the birds at the feeder. Mimi wanders too far but I don't retrieve her.

I just peer over the rim of my coffee mug at a red cedar on the edge of the lawn. At the base of the cedar sits a gray squirrel. I'm about to get Mimi but something stops me. A wildlife drama begins to unfold. Summer languor drops away.

A red fox leaps out from behind the stone wall that borders the woods. Like a panther bursting from jungle cover, it flies toward the red cedar. The fox leaps more than 3 feet high and almost 15 feet laterally (as I will learn from my subsequent measurements). It is about to land on the squirrel. Somehow the squirrel ducks the fox and shoots up the cedar.

Reaching the treetop the squirrel barks repeatedly. For a long moment the fox stands still at the base of the cedar—in bewilderment, I think. It can't believe it has missed. Or is this predator of nocturnal leanings simply dazed by the brightness of day? It is a splendid fox—very tall, weighing perhaps 15 pounds, which is about as big as red foxes get. It acts as if it doesn't see me, even though I stand in the open less than 50 feet away. A human on a coffee break presents no threat.

Finally the fox slips into thickets overhanging the stone wall, but soon it comes back out and trots past the pond. Then it turns right and follows the edge of the wetlands. Before disappearing into a neighbor's yard, it breaks stride and glances into a patch of tall grass bordering the wetlands. I hear a bell and Mimi runs from that patch of grass to the house. The fox must have caught her scent as she hid there, or maybe she hissed when the fox passed. The squirrel is still barking as I gather Mimi up.

The red fox once shared with the raccoon the title of top suburban predator in the East. Now that distinction belongs to the coyote. Long thought of as a symbol of the American West, the coyote has been quietly moving east since the early 20th century. In recent decades it has colonized such far-flung places as Cape Cod, and in 1999 one was captured in New York City's Central Park.

The sprawling suburbs of the East represent a kind of last frontier for the coyote and have been especially hospitable, ecologically speaking. Coyotes do well in habitat where wooded and cleared areas mingle. Many suburban settings have an ample supply of rodents, rabbits, and deer, the mammals coyotes prey on most heavily. Red foxes not only fall victim to coyotes; they also compete with them. This compounding of pressure on the fox's survival may explain why I've had fewer fox sightings as the coyote population has increased.

Possibly the fastest wild canid, the coyote is an opportunistic predator—it views any animal it can catch and subdue as fair game, including pets. With a top speed that can break 40 miles per hour, a coyote can easily run down a cat or small dog, and at 40 pounds a large coyote will have little trouble overpowering the victim. Suburbanites who let their small pets roam flirt with disaster. Smaller livestock are also vulnerable, young sheep in particular. Do coyotes pose a danger to humans? For the answer I went to Matthew Gompper, a mammalogy professor at the University of Missouri and an expert on carnivore ecology.

"Almost all attacks on people seem to represent an attempt to gain or to defend a food resource," he said. Numerous coyote attacks have been documented, especially in the West. Gompper knows of five or six attacks in the Northeast.

"In some of the Northeast cases," he said, "the coyotes were getting handouts or were feeding at dumps, so they were habituated to humans and associated them with food. Other cases involved hunters. Hunters track wounded animals, and so do coyotes, which makes the two more likely to meet. Instances of coyotes viewing humans as prey are extremely rare. In 1998, a coyote attacked a three-year-old boy on Cape Cod. I've seen no conclusive evidence that the coyote was being fed, so this may have been one of the few cases of true predation directed at humans."

Such anomalies notwithstanding, Gompper says that coyotes are less threatening than the dog next door. In his opinion, and in mine, we should feel lucky to see them, which doesn't happen as often as we might expect. Although their population density can be much higher in the suburb than in the forest, coyotes are least active in broad daylight and they tend to steer clear of people. If they do come into view, they're usually written off as dogs.

A bold young male once demonstrated this cloak of invisibility to me. He came trotting across the lawn from a break in the stone wall, veering this way and that before he stopped to stare at all the flitting around my bird feeders. When the coyote turned toward the yard next door I stepped out to watch. A boy was on the deck, shaking out a dust mop. He didn't seem to notice that a coyote was coming down the middle of his yard. When the boy banged the mop on the railing, the coyote flinched and cut back for the stone wall but then reversed direction and crossed into the yard of the neighbor on the other side, disappearing behind a tall hedge.

I hurried to the end of the driveway and peeked around the hedge. By then the coyote was gone. The lady next door was gardening in the far corner of the yard. Had she seen blind to the coyote, too? It was like a movie scene: cut from one suburbanite to another as they go about their daily chores, oblivious to the sinister character who may soon disrupt the neighborhood calm.

A running coyote holds its tail down. Some field guides suggest using this trait to differentiate coyotes from domestic dogs, which run with their tails up. But for me the coyote's wildness makes the best field mark. You can see it in the eyes, especially if you lock gazes with one. There's none of the amiable sparkle that a domestic dog conveys. Coyote eyes have a distant, almost vacant quality.

Birders talk about identifying a bird by its jizz, the unique impression a species gives, even when glimpsed for a fraction of a second. The coyote also has jizz, and much of this is in its self-confident carriage. It lopes along like the great survivor it has proved to be.

We are not the only animal able to recognize coyote jizz. The neighborhood cats can easily distinguish the coyote from its domesticated brethren. They know that the coyote doesn't chase them for fun; the mere appearance of one sends them up a tree or running for home. Birds are even more attuned to coyotes. Crows mob them vociferously and are, therefore, excellent coyote locators. I've heard chickadees, Carolina Wrens, and catbirds voice their contempt in similar fashion. Pet dogs never raise avian alarm to such levels.

The coyote's most frequent prey around my home may be the woodchuck, or groundhog. This dandelion eater is an appealing target. Near the size of a cat, the woodchuck is large enough to feed a family of coyotes, yet it can be easier prey than the cat since it forages in the open and has short legs—good for digging, not so good for running. The woodchuck's wariness compensates for its lack of speed, providing it doesn't wander too far from its burrow.

A blazingly hot April day brought a woodchuck-stalking coyote to the center of the lawn—a tall and thin female who looked very ragged, possibly because she was shedding her winter coat. She had bald spots on her lower back, and her tail was like a rat's, except for a tuft of fur at the tip. With lowered head she stood under the midday sun and moved in ultraslow motion, her muzzle pointed at a woodchuck who foraged unsuspectingly on a neighbor's lawn a good 200 yards away.

I had never seen any dog move so cautiously. She raised each front leg and held it for several seconds, placing it down with the utmost delicacy. Her hind legs followed almost as slowly. At this rate it would have taken an age for her to get close enough to attempt a kill. Seeming to realize this, she quit and lay down. I had slid out with my camera and now snapped pictures from behind the walkway wall. She looked hot and weak but her alertness hadn't flagged. At each click of the shutter she turned her head in my direction.

I stayed low and kept still. She couldn't make me out, though I was much closer to her than she was to the woodchuck. Since dogs don't have highly acute vision, I was surprised that she could identify the woodchuck from such a distance. But she was sensitized to woodchuck jizz, and this one was in the open, a walking hamburger ready for takeout. Maybe she was planning to deliver it to her den, where four to six hungry pups could be waiting.

At first I rooted for the woodchuck. It is a more familiar neighbor. A female lived for years in a burrow next to the front porch. I watched her raise many young and send them forth into the world. The coyote's quarry might have been a descendent. My sympathies, however, soon shifted. The longer I studied the coyote, the more emaciated she became, until I convinced myself she was near starvation. It was at least 90°F under that sun. How could she stand it? Just when I reached the point of neutrality, she gave up. A figure of dejection, she slowly returned to the stone wall and climbed over it into the shady woods. I waited half a minute and followed with my camera.

I stayed on my side of the stone wall and walked along it— down to the pond, then back to where she had climbed over— carefully scanning the woods. When I got to the break in the wall

I saw her. She hadn't given up at all. She'd gone in the direction opposite mine to get closer to the woodchuck under cover of woods. Something had prevented her from carrying out the attack. It might have been the two houses she'd have to pass on the final approach to her prey. Too risky. So now she was coming back to retry Plan A.

She hadn't seen me. I was shielded by the stone wall and heavy underbrush. She'd almost surely come through the break in the wall. This was my chance for a very close photo. I prefocused my telephoto lens on the spot where in seconds she would emerge. The delay seemed too long, so I lowered the camera and looked around. She was still coming but had gotten close enough to notice my subtlest movements. I was busted. She stopped dead and stared. If there's anything that makes coyotes suspicious, it's a person trying to be wily like them.

She stared for only a moment. Then she exploded away in a full gallop, erasing any impression of weakness. She covered the first few yards while glancing over her shoulder at me, and I was flattered to think she needed to confirm that I wasn't following. She ran along the stream bank toward the pond. I swung my lens around and got off two shots as she sailed over rocks and vines and downed trees—shots of blur, it turned out. She was fast, of course, but also graceful, and she fled in near silence. I heard only the suction her feet produced as she pulled them from the mud.

Aside from woodchucks, the coyotes in my neck of suburbia seem to prey heavily on deer, especially fawns, and on young Canada Geese. I'm convinced that deer numbers have declined in recent years, and I think the coyote is responsible. I see fewer deer around the house and in the woods, and fewer lying dead on the roadside. Although Canada Geese in general seem as plentiful as ever, around the house I've noticed that when coyotes are most in evidence, fewer goslings survive to adulthood. I ran my theory by Matthew Gompper. He hasn't come across studies that support it.

"Since coyotes have only recently arrived in eastern suburbs," he said, "we know little about their natural history there. Once researchers have time to study them, we'll be able to make informed comparisons with what has occurred in the West, where coyotes have very different prey and competitors."

If coyotes prove an effective natural control in areas where white-tailed deer and Canada Geese are overpopulated, I wonder if suburbanites will welcome the news. We may be too fond of maligning the coyote as a murderer of pets and as a danger to young children. Rather than live with the coyote, we may want to go on condemning deer for eating our ornamental plants and for having the audacity to collide with our cars.

What will newspaper humorists of scatological leanings do when the Canada Goose ceases to be a "problem species"? I, for one, will not miss their exquisitely detailed accounts of pernicious geese befouling parks and golf courses. There are more amusing ornithological subjects for writers to mine. I found a particularly rich lode in the bird songs of Hollywood, California.

CHAPTER 13

BIRD SONGS OF HOLLYWOOD:
AN UNNATURAL HISTORY

THE WIZARDS OF HOLLYWOOD CAN DUPLICATE A CITY STREET ON A STUDIO back lot, create convincing jungle warfare on a sound stage in Culver City, and dazzle filmgoers with special effects. Technical advisors—scientists, soldiers, doctors, lawyers, computer gurus—ensure that what happens on screen is plausible. And yet, one small but significant aspect of moviemaking is consistently overlooked. Hollywood is tone deaf to the songs of birds.

On movie and television soundtracks, bird songs are often inserted without regard to whether the birds would ordinarily occur in the locale, season, habitat, and time of day depicted in the film. Although bird songs might be picked up by sound recordists as a movie is shot, they are usually added during the postproduction phase to give outdoor scenes "atmosphere." To do the job right, you wouldn't merely cue up "Bird Songs of

North America" and record onto the movie's soundtrack whatever songs strike your fancy. You would choose only songs one could expect to hear in that tiny piece of the world shown in the segment of the film you are editing.

Hollywood sound editors usually are not so particular. A movie set in America containing all the right bird songs is as rare as Kirtland's Warbler. No one seems to have told the moviemakers that birds have geographic ranges (Carolina Wrens can be found singing in New Jersey but are absent from southern California); that birds migrate (the Yellow Warbler pouring out its heart in May departs in fall); and that birds live in certain surroundings (meadowlarks don't vocalize in towering forests).

Hollywood's recklessness in adding bird songs to movie soundtracks is puzzling, considering its obsessive attention to detail in other areas. Special effects teams can spend days shooting complex sequences that look true to life but will last only seconds in the finished film. In period pieces the architecture, furnishings, costumes, props, and customs of the day are painstakingly researched. Sets constructed to mirror actual places are so accurate we believe they are real. Is it any wonder that even modest films cost tens of millions of dollars to produce?

For those of us who watch birds and have learned their songs, however, movies can be maddening, no matter how big their budgets. It's hard for us to concentrate on a story when ornithological incongruities assault our ears. Compounding our frustration is that other people usually don't notice. Either they're not conversant with bird language or they fall under the hypnotic spell of drama and screen out any incidental sounds.

Moviegoers would not believe a film that showed the streets

of New York lined with palm trees. Misplaced bird songs, the aural equivalent of this, fall into eight main categories:

East is East and West is West, Except in Hollywood
On movie soundtracks, I've heard Eastern Screech-Owls and Eastern Bluebirds in California settings. The Eastern Screech-Owl's call added mystery to the opening scene of *E.T.*, but in the movie's suburban California setting, this bird would be no less an alien than Steven Spielberg's lovable space traveler.

The award for the biggest geographic gaffe, however—one that transcended continental boundaries—could go to a recent film adaptation of *Lord of the Flies*. Watching this "lost on a desert island" film, presumably set in the South Pacific, I kept hearing the scream of a Red-tailed Hawk. The moviemakers were particularly fond of this sound, using it repeatedly to symbolize the isolation and vulnerability of a group of schoolboys—the marooned survivors of a plane crash. Yet the Red-tailed Hawk normally occurs only in North America, so either the castaways weren't really lost, or the bird was.

There may be a similar blunder at the end of *The Godfather.* I've seen this great film countless times but only recently noticed something strange in the scene where Al Pacino, as Michael Corleone, confronts his brother-in-law Carlo (played by Gianni Russo) about Sonny Corleone's murder.

"Barzini's dead," says Michael with frightful calmness. "So is Philip Tattaglia, Moe Greene, Strachi, Cuneo. Today I settle all Family business, so don't tell me you're innocent, Carlo. Admit what you did." Carlo weeps.

During this exchange, a crow calls in the background. To me it doesn't sound quite like an American Crow. It sounds more like a carrion crow, which is Eurasian.

Day for Night

For some moviemakers, there is no distinction between diurnal and nocturnal birds. In their films, a robin may burst into song at midnight; an owl may hoot at high noon. If it seems to enhance the mood, they will have the Whip-poor-will calling in bright sun, though it raises its voice chiefly to the moon. In *Eyes Wide Shut,* it's the dead of night as Tom Cruise walks up to the gates of a Long Island mansion, the scene of an orgiastic costume ball. Inexplicably, a Blue Jay—by no means a bird of the night—calls three times. Defenders of Stanley Kubrick's moviemaking may invoke artistic license, but is this just an excuse for biological illiteracy?

Mall of the Wild

The cry of the Common Loon gets a lot of play in the movies. It is a sound I associate with wilderness—large, pristine lakes where humans rarely intrude. In the movies, however, you can hear a loon almost anywhere. The determining factor is fog. A suburban scene with close-cut lawns, water sprinklers, sidewalks, and kids riding bicycles is not good loon habitat, but add some fog and Hollywood will have loons crying from every direction.

Half-baked Alaska

As an L.A. detective on loan to a northern Alaska police department, a sleep-deprived Al Pacino mentors junior officer Hilary Swank and matches wits with a murderous Robin Williams, in *Insomnia*. Despite the fine cast, *Insomnia* is no *Godfather,* and I found my attention wandering. I perked up, however, when I heard a Whooping Crane's call dubbed over a shot of a Great Blue Heron (a species restricted to southeastern Alaska). Director Christopher Nolan, so fastidious in his previous film, the cultish

Memento, can be forgiven. Many people incorrectly say "crane" when they mean "heron," so at least there's method in this bit of movie madness.

Winter of my Discontent

The scene in the television movie is cold and dismal. Snow blankets a dusk-shrouded landscape crossed by picturesque split-rail fences. A man and a woman embrace near the barn. Soon they are serenaded by the celestial fluting of a Hermit Thrush, which many people believe has the most beautiful voice of all North American birds. The thrush sang on and on, but all I could think was that, in all my years of listening to birds, I've never heard a Hermit Thrush sing in winter. Where I live, the song of the Hermit Thrush echoes through deep woods in spring and summer only. So much for willing suspension of disbelief.

The Time Is out of Joint

The cardinal figures prominently in Tim Burton's *Sleepy Hollow.* During the opening credits, Johnny Depp, playing "Constable" Ichabod Crane, releases a caged cardinal as he prepares for an extended visit to the Hudson Valley. In a romantic scene with Depp in the Sleepy Hollow countryside, Christina Ricci (as Katrina Van Tassel) identifies a wild cardinal by its song.

Cardinals were once kept as pets (now an illegal practice), but the ornithological record suggests that a cardinal would not have ordinarily occurred in this film's setting: the New York of 1799. Historically a southern species, the cardinal has spread north into New York, where today it is common, mainly within the past 60 years, probably aided by the proliferation of bird feeders. Bird ranges change over time, another natural fact that is often lost on

Hollywood. Washington Irving's *Legend of Sleepy Hollow,* by the way, never mentions the cardinal.

Silent Spring

It's a beautiful spring morning on film. The sun rises above the hilltops. Warm light streams over the scene. Flowers are in bloom, trees are leafing out, the meadow is a lush green, and the birds are ... mute. The actors populate a world devoid of the wild melodies of seasonal renewal, and no one has told the sound editor. It's Rachel Carson's nightmare come true.

Birding Hot Spots of Hollywood

The converse of the silent-spring technique: In some movies, sound editors go wild over bird songs. To every outdoor scene they attach a litany of singing birds, and you never hear the same one twice. In recording the soundtrack, they seem to have turned on the bird-song tape and left the room. If such a place really existed, birders across America would flock to it. The actors, of course, never notice anything unusual as one bird species after another visits their idyllic hamlet, reciting its sweet strain.

Recently I saw a movie that used the birding hot spot style of sound recording to heighten suspense in a night scene. In quick succession I heard several species of owls, Chuck-will's-widow, Whip-poor-will, and the omnipresent Common Loon. Not only did every nocturnal bird of North America happen to occur in this movie location; each species also sang on cue without stepping on another bird's lines.

Watching a movie with a few family members, I couldn't help pointing out another bird-song error. They answered with a polite smile, a blank stare, and a "Shhh!" I kept quiet and brooded over the error through the rest of the film, longing for the day when Hollywood adds "bird-song specialist" to its roster of technical advisors.

CHAPTER 14

RITES OF PASSAGE

THE END OF A MILD DAY IN EARLY MARCH BRINGS ME TO WAKEMAN'S FARM. Conditions are perfect for viewing the aerial mating display of the American Woodcock. The sun has slid away, and the moon is rising. The air is still and warm, the cornfield wet from melted snow. Muddy tire ruts warn me to leave the car at the edge of the field.

My feet sink a good two inches with each step I take for field's center. Beyond the matted grass of the farm, houses peek through leafless trees, and car noises break the evening silence. With man-made sights and sounds crowding it, the field seems small and vulnerable. But soon it will turn green, and the trees will sprout leaves that screen out the houses and dampen the swishing of cars and the rumble of engines. And then it feels infinitely green and protected, like a field in Vermont.

It is 15 minutes after sunset. The woodcocks should begin their show at any moment. In the Northeast their courtship ritual usually is in full force by early spring, but this stout, long-billed bird is no mere sign of the season. The flight of the woodcock is an avian phenomenon.

It begins at twilight, when the male woodcock moves from woods or thickets to an open area. On the ground, he throws back his head and vibrates his tongue, producing an odd buzz. Once I strapped a flashlight to my camera and photographed this curious behavior. The woodcock strutted a short distance between buzzes, and I was close enough to hear the clucks and gurgles that punctuate his bizarre strumming.

After several buzzes the woodcock leaps into the air, flies slowly on whistling wings, and climbs in wide spirals until he's almost out of sight. Nearing the top of his ascent, he beats his wings into a frenzy, and the whistling reaches a fever pitch. When his wings and his whistling can go no higher, the woodcock bursts into a cascading love song as he seesaws back to earth like a falling leaf. For the last 50 yards he glides in silence. After landing he buzzes again, and if he's lucky a female joins him.

The woodcock repeats this performance for about a half hour, competing with other males. The first male to go up may finish uninterrupted, but his rivals won't wait long. Soon the displays overlap, and for the woodcock's human audience the night becomes a festival. One woodcock takes off as another's flight climaxes. The heavens engulf one bird as a spent performer angles down to the grass. Recently landed birds and those about to fly challenge each other with buzzes. The dimming sky is filled with smudges of motion, and whistling wings electrify the air.

Last year in this field, at least ten males regaled me, the best show I've seen in 25 years of woodcock-watching. They flew on all sides of me and in a neighboring meadow. I whirled around to catch this one flying up, that one gliding down. Coming in for a landing, one woodcock zipped by my head, his wings sounding off softly as he fluttered to a stop. Like tonight, it was clear and warm, and the ground was moist, but there was no moon. Rising behind bare trees, this evening's moon floats pale orange under a veil of cloud.

I keep telling myself it's a perfect night for woodcocks, but there's no sign of them. The calls of White-throated Sparrows draw me from my observation post to thickets at the edge of the field. Listening to the sparrows gather for the night, I stamp my feet in a patch of snow to clean my boots, though I will cross the mud to return to my car.

My attention shifts to the cry of a Killdeer coming across the field. I can't tell whether it's on the ground or in the air. Two quacking Mallard slant across the sky and bank toward a stream. A cardinal sings, a Blue Jay screams but the woodcocks are silent.

Giant spruces on the horizon pierce the orange-bottomed dome of sky. The moon has risen above the trees; fewer White-throated Sparrows call. I play a game with myself. The woodcocks will start in exactly one minute. The second hand of my watch sweeps completely around and ... nothing.

Starting back for the car, I see two figures moving about in the murky distance. Have they seen me? Who are they? I grope at my neck for my binoculars, then realize I left them home because, in the fading light of woodcock-watching, binoculars quickly become excess weight. Getting closer I deliberately step into crunchy snow, and the figures look in my direction—a man and a woman wearing binoculars.

"You must be here to see the woodcocks."

"Yes," the man answers. "Have you seen any?"

"No, and it's getting late. Either something isn't right, or the woodcocks aren't here."

They have never seen the mating display of the woodcock. I tell them they're in for a treat, but not tonight.

The next morning, robins, grackles, and Blue Jays rummage through the leafy slope outside my door. I hear the song of a Red-winged Blackbird. Perhaps there was a flight of migrating birds overnight. Perhaps the woodcock has arrived.

THIS RITE OF SPRING, THE WOODCOCK'S AND MINE, WAS REPEATED EVERY March in the Wakeman's Farm cornfield, and though some years the birds kept me waiting days and even weeks, they never disappointed me. If they were late I had distractions enough. Wakeman's was a place for all seasons.

On warm late winter days in the apple orchard, I would sometimes hear the song of the Eastern Bluebird beckoning spring. For most of one summer, I listened at dawn and dusk to the amusing catcalls of the rare Yellow-breasted Chat and was lucky enough to glimpse this largest of warblers in the tangles west of the cornfield. I saw other rarities, too: Lawrence's Warbler, Upland Sandpiper, Dickcissel, Sandhill Crane. I watched a Sharp-shinned Hawk send a flock of Dark-eyed Juncos scattering; White-throated Sparrows scold a lone screech-owl; a Merlin zoom by like a jet fighter; vengeful crows chase a Red-tailed Hawk. Bullfrogs called from a pond at the farm's southwest end and dodged the dagger bills of Great Blue and Green Herons. White-eyed Vireos, Indigo Buntings, Yellow-billed and Black-billed Cuckoos, and Willow Flycatchers returned to the thickets in summer.

Toward evening in mid-August, the Wood Thrush's wistful melody echoed through the small woodland cathedral, a dirge to the nesting season's end. In September, Common Nighthawks migrating south skimmed the tops of the uncut grass, feasting on flying insects, and Ruby-throated Hummingbirds helicoptered between jewelweed blossoms.

After I moved from Westport to Weston, I could wander in a nature preserve 50 times the size of this farm. But I still visited the place where I had seen so many birds for the first time. For all it offered, the farm was usually deserted, but others eventually discovered it, and they weren't watching birds.

The town of Westport, which acquired the land some years before, had been leasing it to an out-of-town farmer, but the cornfield had fallen idle. Town officials viewed the unplowed land as somehow incomplete and felt compelled to find another use for it. They began pushing to transform the cornfield into athletic fields, with studies showing an athletic-field shortage and with backing from the Little League. Our young athletes are deprived, they argued, and we must build athletic fields even if it means sacrificing the last remaining farm.

I have fond memories growing up playing basketball, stickball, and football, but they fade to insignificance compared with the richness of my experiences in nature. I saw plenty of athletic fields in Westport but only one Wakeman's—it was all that remained of the farmland that once covered much of the town. For me, and for anyone else wishing to explore there, it was a portal to the disappearing world of nature. Replacing the cornfield with a great lawn would drive away or destroy wildlife and demolish a valuable natural classroom. It would kill an old farm.

When their representatives voted to bulldoze the farm into history, most townspeople saw it as progress. Preserving land is fine for tropical rain forests, but not in our backyard. Where do they think migratory birds from the rain forest raise their young? Every spring, birds that spend the winter in Central and South America return to New England's suburbs, nesting on farmland and forgotten patches of nature.

We call such places "undeveloped," an innocuous-sounding term that has crept into the language and created an antinature bias without our knowing it. The term implies that the poor, impaired land needs our help to reach its full potential. But as naturalist David Suzuki has pointed out, from the perspective of the plants and animals living there, this land is fully developed. Nature knows how to make full and wise use of the land, if only we would let it.

After the fate of Wakeman's Farm was sealed, I waited awhile before revisiting the place. By then it had been transformed into athletic fields. Its new name—Wakeman Park— was carved in foot-high letters into a boulder at the entrance to a new parking lot. Empty of people, it was pleasant enough—a flat expanse of trim green bordered by a grandstand and a chain-link fence.

Water pipes and electrical lines had been laid, and a thick layer of smooth blacktop had been pressed over the bumpy dirt driveway. A public telephone stood watch. The pickup truck that rusted for decades near the orchard, almost hidden by weeds, was gone. The old footpath, where I crawled under fallen limbs and squeezed between thorny wild roses, had been widened so much it would have allowed passage of a bus. I thought of Ms. and Sasha, the wonderful dogs who came here with me, each in her time. They loved Wakeman's as much as I did. How puzzled they would be to behold the old farm now.

Untouched land still surrounded the ball field, but that, too, was owned by the town, which undoubtedly would feel compelled to "develop" it. Indeed, town officials were already eyeing an adjacent meadow as the site for a new middle school. Standing there I realized that, whatever remained of the old farm, my heart was no longer with it.

On my way to the car, I saw a female American Kestrel effortlessly winging a few feet above the grass. She alighted on one of the conifers planted to screen the ball players from neighboring houses. I took my spotting scope from the trunk and watched her confidently survey the new landscape, fanning her reddish tail and spreading her wings to keep her balance. Perhaps she was descended from the kestrels I found nesting here years ago and, like me, had come to mark the passing of yet another remnant of the wild.

I was still mourning the loss of Wakeman's Farm when Sherwood Island State Park came under attack. An old Westport mansion, known after its first owner as the Eno house, had been slated for demolition. The present owner planned to build a new house in its place. To save the empty and rundown Eno house, reputedly a fine example of colonial revival architecture, a historic preservation group proposed to move it from the banks of the Saugatuck River to Sherwood Island. They had an ambitious scheme. They would lift the 32-room, 200-foot-long mansion onto a barge. Then they would chug down the Saugatuck River, turn left at Long Island Sound, and plunk their cargo down in the middle of the state park.

The move would take three months and cost 500,000 dollars. Another 1.7 million dollars would be needed to renovate the neglected mansion. The preservation group's members weren't worried about raising the money. They had surmounted their biggest obstacle: finding a plot of land big enough to accommodate the Eno house. Once renovated, the house would become their headquarters. It would also contain a state tourist bureau. The preservation group claimed support from Connecticut's governor and from the Department of Environmental Protection, which oversees state parks. The stewards of public land—those entrusted to defend Sherwood Island, Connecticut's oldest state park—had flung open the gates to an invading force.

To placate local environmental organizations, the preservation group offered them space in the Eno house. I was a member of one such organization. We were slow to fight, so I broke away. At first I was a lone renegade, but soon I found others who shared my outrage, and the war over Sherwood Island began.

We fought on several fronts. The propaganda war raged in the local papers, which played up the environmentalist versus preservationist theme. We went to public hearings, and we used the Freedom of Information Act to gather intelligence. There was intrigue: Private letters I sent to public officials fell into enemy hands; some of the enemy's confidential documents found their way to me. I received a late night phone call from a stranger who described himself as an architectural history buff. He wouldn't say how, but he had gained entry into the locked Eno house. "It's in bad shape," he confided, "and historically it's not all that significant."

A month into the war I dropped my nuclear bomb. While the preservationists were distracted in Westport, slugging it out with us in the local papers, I wrote an op-ed piece for the *Hartford Courant*. All the sound and fury in Westport didn't matter, I reasoned. The decision-makers were in Hartford, the state capital.

If I could make a convincing enough argument, maybe the people with real power would nix the Eno move.

The piece pointed to my Sherwood Island bird checklist, which compiles 15 years of data on the seasonal abundance of more than 280 species and testifies to the park's ecological value. You don't move buildings into a park, I argued, especially not a palatial building like the Eno house into a relatively small and environmentally sensitive park like Sherwood Island—the only coastal state park in Fairfield County. Would we entertain for a moment the notion of lowering such a monster into the Grand Canyon?

"Winkler's likening of Sherwood Island to the Grand Canyon is absurd," wrote the president of the preservation group in a letter to the editor. When I read the letter I thought, well it's the Grand Canyon to me. That same week, the Connecticut Department of Environmental Protection concluded that moving the Eno house to Sherwood Island "would not be feasible." The preservation group failed to find an alternate site, and six months later the Eno house was demolished.

It was a Pyrrhic victory, however, at least for me. More than six years since the Eno debacle, I can't visit Sherwood Island without being flooded by unpleasant memories. When the preservationists marched in, many people who had professed affection for the park didn't want to get involved. Conflict seemed to make them uncomfortable. You can't choose a side and still please everybody, so they sat on the fence, and when it was all over they acted as if nothing had happened. If we had presented a united front, and fought hard, the war would have been won in days rather than weeks.

The near loss of Sherwood Island taught me that no part of the suburban wilderness is sacred. You become fond of a place at your own risk. One day you could find it divided into housing lots. You might win a battle, but your enemy will be back. He's eyeing the Sherwood Islands of the world right now.

I slowly keep moving and stay just ahead of the destruction, like the bulldozer-driven deer. My present stop is Newtown. For my money it's the best town in Fairfield County, with its comparative bounty of untamed land. There are enough ramshackle houses to give the place character, and now, in summer, the wild sections are at their jungly best. The people here seem better for all this—more relaxed than those in lower Fairfield County, not always trying to cut in front of you at the four-way stop.

In the few years I've lived here, however, I've seen the troubling signs: dirt roads paved, old fields turned to landscaping for fat houses, motorists grown tense, state forests scarred with the tracks of all-terrain vehicles. There's no future anywhere in Fairfield County, I often think. But then I'll drive along Route 136 late at night—no headlights on the back of my neck, good songs on the radio, the deep woods of the reservoir watershed unfolding on either side of me—and the optimist in me soars.

Although I view the suburb with ambivalence, I'll always believe in the glory of its wild places. With each chipping away of them, our neighborhoods become less livable. The suburban wilderness is where birders, nature writers, and environmentalists are made. Life may take us farther afield, but this is where the adventures begin.

EPILOGUE

ON A SUMMER EVENING I WAS CAUGHT IN THE CROSSFIRE OF DUELING Wood Thrushes, each defending his portion of the forest. Their chosen weapons were their voices; melodies were their ammunition. Each sought to wound the other's pride, but their sweet fluting pierced only the evening silence. I was moved, but both Wood Thrushes stood their ground.

I doubt that the duelists saw one another, because the Wood Thrush is content to pour out his nocturne from the middle of a low limb draped by leaves. He needs no approving audience and can project his voice without resorting to a singing perch in the treetop. The brown-backed, speckle-breasted, eight-inch Wood Thrush only looks drab. All of his beauty is concentrated in his voice. Let the Scarlet Tanager take the prize as the forest's flashiest dresser. Among his winged brethren, the song of the Wood Thrush has no equal.

He sings more enchantingly than any bird I know. Lyrical, liquid, and loud, his voice has beauty and depth to match nature's. On the trail, I often find myself stopping to admire the Wood Thrush's gift.

After wintering mainly in Mexico and Central America, Wood Thrushes return north to breed. The male's echoing melody challenges his rivals, wakes the raccoon, and serenades the woodland sojourner. In California they don't hear Wood Thrushes, which in summer occur only in the eastern forest. It's enough to prevent me from moving West.

His singular talent won this common bird the unabashed affection of two of America's foremost naturalists, an artist and a writer. While traveling in Europe, John James Audubon got homesick for "the sweet melodious strains of that lovely recluse, my greatest favorite, the Wood Thrush." Henry David Thoreau said, "He touches a depth in me which no other bird's song does," and he called the wood thrush "a Shakespeare among birds."

Ancient magic lives on in the woods. You can go there and hear what Audubon and Thoreau heard, the same song Native Americans heard in the virgin forest. The Pilgrims must have heard it, too, and perhaps the Wood Thrush comforted them in their wild new world.

The Wood Thrush's song consists of several phrases, variations on his basic *ee-o-lay* theme, in quality like a flute but richer, not airy. Each phrase usually concludes with a high-pitched chord. Throaty utterings audible at close range may introduce the next phrase. The song's ending is sometimes marked by a downsliding note that slows and trails off. After a pause, the song is repeated. Occasionally, the Wood Thrush launches into a series of sustained intonations, a haunting counterpoint to his primary song.

There is wide variation in the singing ability of Wood Thrushes. Some are almost mechanical, others merely sweet—the inspired Wood Thrush sings with a certain soulfulness. He plays his fine vocal instrument with great sweetness, yet there is an undercurrent of sadness. He speaks to me of struggle and survival, of loss and rebirth, and ultimately of hope. He awakens me to the indefinable yearnings that humans and Wood Thrushes share.

The thrushes, a family that includes the American Robin and the Eastern Bluebird, are known for their vocal skill. Some have argued that the Wood Thrush's close relative, the Hermit Thrush, is the better singer, but the Hermit Thrush's ethereal song strikes me as too heavenly. The voice of the Wood Thrush, touched by Earthly matters, resonates more powerfully with the human condition.

He can sing with such feeling and musical sophistication, yet we call him a wild animal. Is it the older birds who sing best, their voices having mellowed with time, or does a special gene make certain Wood Thrushes exceptional? Of course, the tones most soothing to my ears may grate the nerves of other Wood Thrushes, and the singers I pass up may be the envy of their clan.

A widespread species, the Wood Thrush can be heard from a suburban yard if there is a woodlot nearby, but I seek better acoustics. To fully appreciate the forest's supreme melody, go to the forest, where traffic noise, mowers, hammering, and human voices barely penetrate. In the Wood Thrush's preferred concert hall of moist woods, every leaf seems to serve as his sound reflector, imparting bell-like reverberations to his clear, round notes.

Although he sings early in the morning and periodically throughout the day, my favorite time to escape the droning suburb and receive the Wood Thrush's soothing strains is when the warm light of a summer day fades. As other birds are piping their last notes, the voice of the Wood Thrush suddenly rises. Soon his song rules, and the woods, though not really silent, seem so except for this bird, because his sonorous voice commands attention.

For singing Wood Thrushes, summer ends early. Although they remain in my part of New England through September, by mid-August most of them have fallen silent. Perhaps the most stirring Wood Thrush I ever heard was singing late in the season. It was a warm day, but it hinted of fall, and I felt summer slipping away.

An orange haze filtered through the trees from where the Wood Thrush sang. To gaze on this pleasant light, to be bathed in it, to see the large trees reaching high into the air, their leaves hanging motionless, and to hear his ageless song rising above it all—this put me in a state of almost hypnotic serenity.

I never saw this Wood Thrush. I wonder what he was feeling as he sang his rhapsody in blue. I can only imagine that he was bidding the summer farewell and voicing a message of hope for summers to come.